THE
SUPREME COURT
CRISIS

A Da Capo Press Reprint Series

FRANKLIN D. ROOSEVELT
AND THE ERA OF THE NEW DEAL

GENERAL EDITOR: FRANK FREIDEL

Harvard University

THE
SUPREME COURT
CRISIS

By

MERLO J. PUSEY

DA CAPO PRESS · NEW YORK · 1973

Library of Congress Cataloging in Publication Data

Pusey, Merlo John, 1902-
    The Supreme Court crisis.
    (Franklin D. Roosevelt and the era of the New Deal)
    Bibliography: p.
    1. United States. Supreme Court. 2. Roosevelt,
Franklin Delano, Pres. U.S., 1882-1945. I. Title.
II. Series.
KF8742.P87   1973   347'.73'26209   74-171699
ISBN 0-306-70389-0

This Da Capo Press edition of *The Supreme Court
Crisis* is an unabridged republication of the first
edition published in New York in 1937. It is
reprinted with permission from a copy in the collection
of the Alderman Library, University of Virginia.

Published by Da Capo Press, Inc.
A Subsidiary of Plenum Publishing Corporation
227 West 17th Street, New York, New York 10011

THE SUPREME COURT CRISIS

THE MACMILLAN COMPANY
NEW YORK · BOSTON · CHICAGO · DALLAS
ATLANTA · SAN FRANCISCO

MACMILLAN & CO., LIMITED
LONDON · BOMBAY · CALCUTTA
MELBOURNE

THE MACMILLAN COMPANY
OF CANADA, LIMITED
TORONTO

THE
SUPREME COURT
CRISIS

By

MERLO J. PUSEY

NEW YORK
THE MACMILLAN COMPANY
1937

PRINTED IN THE UNITED STATES OF AMERICA
BY THE STRATFORD PRESS, INC., NEW YORK

FOREWORD

IN THIS small volume, with penetrating insight and unusual clarity of expression, Mr. Pusey has succeeded in laying bare every material consideration involved in President Roosevelt's startling proposal that Congress authorize him to add six members to the Supreme Court, unless that number of present judges can be coerced into leaving the bench. By making available to all thoughtful citizens, at the very time when the controversy is at white heat, a simple, concise, yet complete summary of the issues which are being debated in every corner of the land, the author has rendered a service of commanding value.

It cannot too often be emphasized that this is not a battle between the President and the Court. Rather it is the President against the people. The Court is brought into the struggle only because the people have charged it with the responsibility of protecting them from the danger of having the executive and the legislative departments attempt to exercise powers beyond those which the people have thus far been willing to trust those governing bodies to have.

One reading of these eleven short chapters will suffice to show that the issue to be decided is whether the people shall continue to have the pro-

FOREWORD

tection of an independent judiciary. For no one can close the volume without the full realization that what the President proposes is to make all judges dependent upon the will of the Executive. Because the Court has restricted the President and the Congress in the exercise of some powers, and it is feared may continue to do so, the plan is to add enough members to make sure of a different result.

It is shown beyond doubt that deception of the unwary was attempted by the talk of relieving congestion and removing the alleged menace of age. The proposal is without valid precedent, nor can it be sustained on the false theory that it is an effort to unpack the Court in response to a claimed mandate from the people. The plea, that an impending crisis justifies hasty action in the nature of a short-cut to an undisclosed goal, is completely refuted.

The average reader will lay down this volume with renewed conviction that American traditions are worth preserving, that it is the spirit of the Constitution that gives it life, and that only a Supreme Court, independent and unawed, stands guard to protect the rights and liberties of the people. If a million American men and women could receive today the message contained within the two covers of this book, the Supreme Court would be saved from pillage.

EDWARD R. BURKE
UNITED STATES SENATOR—NEBRASKA

CONTENTS

THE SUPREME COURT CRISIS

I.

THE PRESIDENT'S DILEMMA

The basis of our political system is the right of the people to make and alter their constitution of government at will.
—George Washington

No GOVERNMENTAL issue since the "tragic era" following the Civil War has caused more thorough soul-searching on the part of the United States than the proposal to remodel the Supreme Court. The people as well as their representatives are aware of the fact that a dramatic chapter in our history is being written. Indeed, they are helping to write it. Street-corner discussions, arguments at restaurant tables, a seemingly endless stream of radio addresses and newspaper reports, protracted hearings before the Senate Judiciary Committee and animated congressional debates are sufficient evidence that our national conscience has been deeply stirred.

There is good reason to believe that President Roosevelt did not realize, when he struck at our so-called "static judiciary," that he would shatter a hornet's nest. His dramatic move came at a moment when he occupied a position of leadership almost unprecedented in the United States. Throughout four years of struggle with the forces

1

of depression he had consistently held the support of large majorities in both houses of Congress. The people had just registered overwhelming approval of his policies. No doubt he expected his remarkable popularity to carry the country with him along the proposed short-cut to new federal power. But his most energetic and courageous supporters were first to balk. Within an incredibly short time after he had crushed his political opposition the President thus found himself in the midst of a fight that overshadows every other event in his career. Politics had been set aside for a good, old-fashioned constitutional scrap.

The first significant aspect of this fight is that it undercuts most of the plans and hopes of the New Deal. To President Roosevelt, packing the Supreme Court is merely the quickest means of achieving a desirable end. It is but a preliminary step to what the President regards as essential control over farming, working conditions and other major economic problems which he believes to be national in scope. But the step he advised Congress to take is of such a dangerous character that it has almost completely diverted attention from the social and economic program it is designed to facilitate. Instead of uniting political groups to promote recovery and set up safeguards against inflation, the President has divided the country by a revolutionary proposal. To economic uncertainty has been added fears that our system of government may be in danger.

As in the case of every great clash of ideas, there are two viewpoints to be considered. No one can deny that a large part of the President's legislative program had been upset by adverse decisions of the Supreme Court. His most far-reaching "new instruments of public power" had been impaled upon the logic of justices appointed by previous Chief Executives. In spite of that handicap, he had renewed and extended his pledge to promote the welfare of many groups by national action. At the very beginning of the second New Deal, therefore, it was apparent that Mr. Roosevelt had promised more than he could deliver with existing federal authority. The voters had instructed him, in a vague, general way, to go ahead with his plans. But in order to do so he had to find some means of breaking through what appeared to be a blockade of judicial decisions.

To appreciate the scope of the President's dilemma we have only to glance at some of the constitutional restraints which the courts had felt obligated to invoke. The technique of the New Deal had been based almost entirely upon the exercise of untried national power to cope with extraordinary economic conditions. As soon as test cases reached the Supreme Court the broad regulatory powers assumed by the Administration were sharply deflated. Both agriculture and local business were removed from the domain of federal agencies attempting to regulate output, prices, etc. Even the special problem industries were held to lie beyond the reach of national planning. And the power of the States to deal with economic problems appeared to be very narrowly limited.

In none of these historic opinions did the Supreme Court attempt to draw a circle around "interstate commerce" or the respective powers of Congress and the States. But it most emphatically recognized a barrier of distinction between "purely local" business—mining, manufacturing and similar pursuits—and the shipment of goods across State lines. Especially in the Guffey Coal Act decision there was a most positive denial of any federal power in the interstate commerce clause "to regulate industry within the State." That did not appear to leave the Administration much latitude in which to work out a national economic program based on this particular segment of the Constitution.

Likewise the Court insisted that the "general welfare" clause—in which New Deal attorneys had discovered hidden treasures of power—is still the same shabby morsel of verbiage that was penned by the Founding Fathers. The Framers' Convention, said the majority in their opinion on the Guffey Coal Act, "made no grant of authority to Congress to legislate substantively for the general welfare, . . . and no such authority exists, save as the general welfare may be promoted by the exercise of the powers which are granted."

Beyond this, the Court emphatically proclaimed its unwillingness to subject the Constitution to any opportunistic stretching. One paragraph from Chief Justice Charles Evans Hughes' partially concurring opinion in *Carter* v. *Carter Coal Co.* sets forth this pointed advice:

4

THE PRESIDENT'S DILEMMA

If the people desire to give Congress the powers to regulate industries within the State and the relations of employers and employes within those industries, they are at liberty to declare their will in the appropriate manner, but it is not for the Court to amend the Constitution by judicial decision.

Adherence to this traditional policy seemed to block the type of recovery program to which the Administration was committed. Mr. Roosevelt refused to discard those projects that were nearest to his heart. And yet he was not prepared to seek a constitutional amendment. So he followed the path of least resistance. In other words, he ignored his grave problem of securing broader national powers throughout the period of his re-election campaign. Then, after he had won a sweeping victory, he chose what he apparently considered the easiest way out.

The President's mind had been playing upon the problem ever since he denounced the N.R.A. decision as a product of the "horse and buggy days." Thousands of suggestions as to what should be done had been sent him from all parts of the country. These had been carefully sorted with the object of discovering some easy method of obtaining authority denied the Administration as a result of Supreme Court opinions. Apparently the whole problem was studied from the viewpoint of making the President's program effective in the shortest possible time. Adaptation of the plan to the established customs of American democracy was a secondary thought.

5

Before leaving on his South American trip the President asked Attorney General Homer S. Cummings and Solicitor General Stanley Reed to select the most promising suggestions for further study. On his return, these proposals were subjected to detailed scrutiny. Finally, they were put through a process of elimination. As a result of that procedure all thought of a constitutional amendment appears to have been abandoned. The Administration's strategists feared that there might be disagreement as to the scope and wording of any amendment proposed, with consequent delay in its ratification.

Turning to its list of legislative proposals, the inner White House circle threw out most of the suggestions because of grave doubts as to their constitutionality. In the end the plan to enlarge the membership of the Supreme Court was the only one left. It had the virtue of violating only the spirit and not the letter of the Constitution. So it was adopted.

It is interesting to note the evolution of the President's thought on the subject. In May, 1935, following the decision against the N.R.A. he declared:

The people have got to decide—not this autumn or this winter, but over a period of five or ten years—if they are going to relegate to the States control of social, economic and working conditions.

There was widespread sympathy with this attitude, despite the resentment aroused by the President's less dispassionate remarks relative to the Supreme Court. The United States today is a very different country from the aggregation of thirteen colonies for which the American charter of 1787 was originally adopted. An increasing number of our modern economic and social problems seem to call for a larger degree of control by the Federal Government. In any event, our political institutions must be frequently examined during periods of changing civilization to determine whether they are continuing to function efficiently in the public interest. The Nation's experience over 150 years indicates that occasional modifications are not only desirable, but indispensable.

At the beginning of the contest, therefore, President Roosevelt had a strong case. His experience in the White House had convinced him that a new relationship between the Government and private enterprise was desirable. Being a man of action by nature, he had courageously sought to meet every emergency, even though many situations seemed to require legislation of a type never before enacted in this country. In short, he had gone as far as he could go, under the policies he had chosen, toward setting the machinery of recovery into motion. He had been checkmated by the Constitution as interpreted by the Supreme Court. And he had indicated a willingness to submit the resulting issue to the people, with plenty of time for a deliberate decision. That commendable attitude undoubtedly helps to account for the Roosevelt landslide of 1936.

THE SUPREME COURT CRISIS

Thus the way was open for realistic consideration of a most vital issue, without condemning the
New Deal, the Constitution, or the Supreme
Court's interpretation of that document. By no
stretch of the imagination can Mr. Roosevelt be
held responsible for the evolution of organized
society or the changed techniques of industry
which call for corresponding adjustment of our
political systems. Nor, on the other hand, can the
Supreme Court be rationally criticized for any element of obsolescence in our 150-year-old charter,
which that body is sworn to uphold. This willingness to recognize the problem as one of national
growth outrunning national power aroused hope
that a constructive solution might be found entirely in keeping with American tradition.

But when the election was safely over, and the
popularity of the President indisputably established, he concluded that it would take too long to
let the people decide their own destiny. He would
direct that decision himself. By simply asking Congress to provide six places on the supreme bench
for justices holding Rooseveltian views of the Constitution he could immediately exercise the powers
sought.

It is this shift of attitude which has aroused the
resentment of so many Democratic legislators who
helped to send Mr. Roosevelt to the White House
for a second term. They, too, are eager to see new
social and economic legislation enacted. But they
are not willing to confuse desirable ends with dictatorial means. Whether the 1937 judiciary bill is

enacted into law or rejected by an irate Senate, therefore, it will doubtless be recorded in history as the most serious mistake of President Roosevelt's brilliant political career.

II.

A CASE BUILT ON SAND

The addition to our number has most sensibly affected our facility as well as the rapidity of doing business. . . . We found ourselves often involved in long and very tedious debates. I verily believe, that if there were twelve judges we should do no business at all or at least very little.

—Justice Joseph Story

To UNDERSTAND the early trends of the controversy over the Supreme Court it is necessary to examine the insulation in which the President packed his bombshell before sending it to Congress. Instead of bluntly asking for authority to appoint new justices who could be expected to interpret the Constitution in harmony with the President's wishes, he evasively proposed an extensive reorganization of our judicial system. His message of February 5 gave the distinct impression that its foremost purpose was to enhance the working efficiency of the courts.

Congress was informed that "one of its definite duties" is "constantly to maintain the effective functioning of the federal judiciary." The President sketched a dark picture of delay and consequent injustice in the courts. To this Attorney General Cummings added a few deft touches that were decidedly out of harmony with the annual re-

10

port of his own department. More judges were said to be needed to relieve the pressure of congested dockets. "Even at the present time," Mr. Roosevelt wrote, "the Supreme Court is laboring under a heavy burden." His argument along that line reached a climax with this declaration: "My desire is to strengthen the administration of justice and to make it a more effective servant of public need."

So far as this policy applied to the lower courts, some of which are seriously congested, a very favorable impression was created. Likewise, Mr. Roosevelt's suggestion that a proctor be appointed to regulate the flow of litigation through the courts in a systematic manner received hearty indorsement. And no one took exception to his request for a law forbidding federal courts to hand down decisions, judgments or injunctions in cases involving constitutional questions "without previous and ample notice to the Attorney General and an opportunity for the United States to present evidence and be heard." But these proposed improvements are not directly related to the issue of remaking the Supreme Court. They were used to camouflage a scheme that the President must have known would be distasteful to Congress and the people.

Of course, the message was not devoid of hints as to the President's real motive. At one juncture he declared: "A constant and systematic addition of younger blood will vitalize the courts and better equip them to recognize and apply the essential concepts of justice in the light of the needs and the

11

facts of an ever-changing world." And his con-
cluding sentence struck this candid note:

If these measures achieve their aim, we may be relieved of the necessity of considering any fundamental
changes in the powers of the courts or the Constitution
of our government—changes which involve consequences so far-reaching as to cause uncertainty as to
the wisdom of such course.

But that anticipated result was made to appear
as merely a by-product of a constructive plan designed to end congestion and delay in the courts.
It was plainly evident that the President did not
want to meet the naked issue of changing the Constitution through executive influence upon the
judiciary. As the controversy progressed, however,
he paid a high price for what Senator Edward R.
Burke called his "surpassingly cunning and deceptive program to discredit the Supreme Court in
the minds of the people."

Ordinarily there would be no objection to the
President applying a chocolate-fudge coating to a
bitter legislative pill. But in this case some ingredi-
ents of the coating went sour and thus left the
entire issue the more unpalatable. Consider, for
example, the statement that the Supreme Court
is so overburdened with work that it cannot review
all the cases properly laid before it. In his message of February 5 the President said:

If petitions in behalf of the Government are excluded, it appears that the Court permitted private
litigants to prosecute appeals in only 108 cases out of

803 applications. Many of the refusals were doubtless warranted. But can it be said that full justice is achieved when a Court is forced by the sheer necessity of keeping up with its business to decline, without even an explanation, to hear 87 per cent of the cases presented to it by private litigants?

It seems clear, therefore, that the necessity of relieving present congestion extends to the enlargement of the capacity of all the federal courts.

A short time before this was written, however, the President's own Solicitor General, Stanley Reed, had noted in his annual report to Congress that there is no congestion of cases in the Supreme Court. That fact is verified by every informed student of the Court's activities, including the President's friend and adviser, Mr. Felix Frankfurter. If any doubt remained, it was completely shattered by the letter of Chief Justice Charles Evans Hughes which was read into the record of the Senate Judiciary Committee's hearings by Senator Burton K. Wheeler. "The Supreme Court is fully abreast of its work," the Chief Justice wrote simply. "We shall be able to hear all these cases [the cases then pending], and such others as may come up for argument, before our adjournment for the term. There is no congestion of cases upon our calendar."

But is the Court rejecting cases to keep its dockets clear, as the President charged? Here, also, the report of the Solicitor General is enlightening. He fully approved the Court's policy, made possible by an act of Congress in 1925, of limiting appeals through writs of certiorari "to important questions of general application" and to "the settlement of conflicts in the decisions of other courts." Indeed, he went on to declare:

The limitations of the Court's statutory jurisdiction and its rules for the exercise of its discretionary jurisdiction should be more carefully observed. Many petitions for writs of certiorari are filed which in the light of settled practice must be regarded as entirely without merit.

No case may be carried to the highest court of the land as a matter of right on the part of the litigants. Congress has decided that where the law is clear individual rights can be adequately protected by review of lower court decisions in the Circuit Courts of Appeals. That is an entirely reasonable policy. For, as Chief Justice Hughes pointed out in his letter to Senator Wheeler, "no single court of last resort, whatever the number of judges, could dispose of all the cases which arise in this vast country and which litigants would seek to bring up if the right of appeal were unrestricted."

When private cases reach the Supreme Court, therefore, it is because they involve a question of public interest. Sometimes a review is granted to resolve conflicts in the decisions of different Circuit Courts of Appeals, to determine constitutional questions, to settle the interpretation of a statute or decide an important question of law. To employ the direct words of the Chief Justice again: "Review by the Supreme Court is thus in the interest of the law, its appropriate exposition and enforcement, not in the mere interest of the litigants."

In following this policy, however, the Court has leaned backward to avoid the rejection of any cases involving a public interest. Petitions for certiorari are granted if four, or in some cases even two or three, justices believe that review is desirable. "I think that it is the view of the members of the Court," said the Chief Justice, "that if any error is made in dealing with these applications, it is on the side of liberality." The statement of Solicitor General Reed previously quoted indicates that the Department of Justice, in its more deliberate moments, concurs in that opinion.

Once an understanding of the Supreme Court's function and procedure is established, the deceptive nature of the President's message becomes obvious. He built his case for enlargement of the Court's membership upon a false premise. Nor was the taint of official camouflage restricted to the activities of the highest court. Upon investigation of Department of Justice records, Mr. Franklyn Waltman, of *The Washington Post,* found that court dockets were in arrears on July 30, 1936, in thirty-four federal judicial districts. But in only four of these districts were the judges more than 70 years of age. He likewise pointed out that there is no relationship between increasing congestion and the age of justices in the Circuit Courts of Appeals. The fiction that senile judges are obstructing the machinery of justice seems to have been invented solely for the purpose of ousting six justices on the

15

Supreme Court who have been too active to please the President.

The natural result of this artifice was a deep feeling of resentment among a considerable body of the President's followers. They felt that they had been tricked. From the very beginning this feeling stiffened their opposition and encouraged relentless analysis of every phase of the judiciary measure. Indeed, the original misrepresentation of the real issue seems to have accounted, in large measure, for the strength the opposition was able to muster.

Attention soon turned, therefore, to the nature of the President's remedy for alleged defects in the judicial system. His message had emphasized the advanced age of some jurists as one cause for the unsatisfactory operation of the courts. Twenty-five of the country's 237 permanent life-tenure judgeships, he pointed out, are occupied by men over 70 years of age. The President feared that the "lowered mental or physical vigor" of aged judges leads them to avoid "examination of complicated and changed conditions." "Older men," he continued, "assuming that the scene is the same as it was in the past, cease to explore or inquire into the present or the future."

It was this reasoning which led him "earnestly" to recommend the enactment of legislation that would provide for "the appointment of additional judges in all federal courts, without exception, where there are incumbent judges of retirement age who do not choose to retire or to resign." Of course, this device was aimed principally at the Supreme Court which had, among its membership of nine, six justices over 70 years of age. But even if the Supreme Court were lagging in its work, the effect of such a transformation would be to make it less and not more efficient.

Long before Chief Justice Hughes penned his devastating letter investigators had called attention to the fact that the Court works as a unit. The thousands of petitions for review submitted to that tribunal are not apportioned among the justices. All of them participate in every decision handed down, unless some member should be disqualified or unable to act in a given case. That is why Mr. Hughes, with the support of both the liberal and conservative members of the bench, so emphatically insisted that, so far as effective operation is concerned, the Court is large enough. His reasoning on this point seems to be incontrovertible:

An increase in the number of justices of the Supreme Court, apart from any question of policy, which I do not discuss, would not promote the efficiency of the Court. It is believed that it would impair that efficiency so long as the Court acts as a unit. There would be more judges to hear, more judges to confer, more judges to discuss, more judges to be convinced and to decide.

Incidentally, the Chief Justice touched upon another point that has been generally overlooked. As a rule middle-aged men have more energy than septuagenarians. But, in regard to efficiency, will a few years' difference in age offset the advantages of long experience in reducing constitutional issues to their essence? When Mr. Hughes said, "It must also be remembered that justices who have been dealing with such matters for years have the aid of long and varied experience in separating the chaff from the wheat," he was merely trying to show that the justices are equal to the onerous task imposed upon them. But the general significance of his words ought not to be lost at a time when such a premium is being placed upon "new blood" behind judicial benches.

The "new blood" argument invites further analysis. Apparently the President won considerable support for his bill by contending that judges should not be permitted to continue on the bench, after old age may have weakened their minds, without the assistance of younger men. Judges who cling to their posts, like the last leaf on the tree, have occasionally raised serious problems. Certainly such men should be encouraged to retire under the liberal arrangement recently made by Congress. Perhaps an age limit for active service on the bench would be desirable. But that would require a constitutional amendment and is therefore excluded from a place in the President's program. Only expedient measures dealing with this issue seem to be welcome at the White House.

Yet the President talks as if he had offered a permanent device for rejuvenation of the courts. The idea he holds out before the people seems to be best expressed in the following quotation from his fireside radio broadcast on the night of March 9:

By bringing into the judicial system a steady and continuing stream of new and younger blood, I hope, first, to make the administration of all federal justice speedier and, therefore, less costly; secondly, to bring to the decision of social and economic problems younger men who have had personal experience and contact with modern facts and circumstances under which average men have to live and work.

It does not appear possible, however, that the bill he submitted to Congress could serve that purpose. A glance at the first two paragraphs of that measure will indicate the discrepancy:

Be it enacted by the Senate and House of Representatives of the United States of America in Congress assembled, That (a) when any judge of a court of the United States, appointed to hold its office during good behavior, has heretofore or hereafter attained the age of seventy years and has held a commission or commissions as judge of any such court or courts at least ten years, continuously or otherwise, and within six months thereafter has neither resigned nor retired, the President, for each such judge who has not so resigned or retired, shall nominate, and by and with the advice and consent of the Senate, shall appoint one additional judge to the court to which the former is commissioned: *Provided,* That no additional judge shall be appointed hereunder if the judge who is of retirement age dies, resigns, or retires prior to the nomination of such additional judge.

(b) The number of judges of any court shall be permanently increased by the number appointed thereto under the provisions of subsection (a) of this section. No more than fifty judges shall be appointed thereunder, nor shall any judge be so appointed if such appointment would result in (1) more than 15 members of the Supreme Court of the United States, (2) more than two additional members so appointed to a circuit court of appeals, the Court of Claims, the United States Court of Customs and Patent Appeals, or the Customs Court, or (3) more than twice the number of judges now authorized to be appointed for any district or, in the case of judges appointed for more than one district, for any such group of districts.

Since the bill was introduced Justice Willis Van Devanter has retired. If none of the other justices should die or retire, five new justices would be appointed under this arrangement, and the membership of the Supreme Court would be permanently fixed at fourteen. After that no "new blood" could be added, except when vacancies might occur. Of course, the additional justices, as Mr. Raymond Moley has pointed out, would become old and might "wear glasses fitted to the needs of another generation," to the acute disgust of some future President. Indeed, there is a possibility that all of the fourteen justices might attain threescore years and ten at some future date. And the President would find it impossible to "reinvigorate" the supreme bench, without obtaining from Congress authority to pack the Court once more.

In view of this provision in the bill, the President's talk about "bringing into the judicial system a steady and continuing stream of new and younger blood" is more fiction than fact. The operation he has proposed is more comparable to a single transfusion to be administered for the specific purpose of accentuating the consanguinity of the Supreme Court to the Chief Executive. That is a special privilege which no self-governing people can afford to grant.

III.

MR. JUSTICE ROOSEVELT

*The attacks upon the Court are merely an expression of the
unrest that seems to wonder vaguely whether law and order pay.*
—Justice Oliver Wendell Holmes

SEVERAL weeks were required to strip the President's judiciary bill of its camouflage. But the job
was done so thoroughly—in the Senate, in the press
and over the air—that the President finally dropped
the artificial tone of his message to Congress. In his
address at the Democratic Victory Dinner in Washington the night of March 4 he launched a trenchant attack upon the Supreme Court. The character of his appeal for popular support in an
outright assault upon the Court can best be illustrated by brief excerpts taken at random:

But economic freedom for the wage earner and the
farmer and the small business man will not wait, like
emancipation, for 40 years. It will not wait for four
years. It will not wait at all . . .
Democracy in many lands has failed for the time
being to meet human needs. People have become so
fed up with futile debate and party bickerings over
methods that they have been willing to surrender
democratic processes and principles in order to get
things done. They have forgotten the lessons of history that the ultimate failures of dictatorship cost

humanity far more than any temporary failures of democracy. . . .

We tried to establish machinery to adjust the relations between the employer and employe.

And what happened?

You know who assumed the power to veto, and did veto that program . . .

Here is one-third of a Nation ill-nourished, ill-clad, ill-housed—Now!

Here are thousands upon thousands of farmers wondering whether next year's prices will meet their mortgage interest—Now!

Here are thousands upon thousands of men and women laboring for long hours in factories for inadequate pay—Now!

Here are thousands upon thousands of children who should be at school, working in mines and mills—Now!

Here are strikes more far-reaching than we have ever known, costing millions of dollars—Now!

Here are spring floods threatening to roll again down our river valleys—Now!

Here is the dust bowl beginning to blow again—Now!

If we would keep faith with those who had faith in us, if we would make democracy succeed, I say we must act—Now!

In this address the President forgot his ideal of judicial reform. He spoke as a protagonist engaged in a bitter fight. It was not justice that concerned him then, but an immediate exercise of power, which the Supreme Court has declared to lie beyond the authority of the Federal Government. Here the real issue was presented in a way that can not possibly be misunderstood.

Widespread reaction against the Victory Dinner address apparently caused the President again to shift his ground. At any rate, he adopted a much more conciliatory tone and a very different line of argument in his so-called fireside chat by radio on the night of March 9. His chief contention this time was that the Supreme Court has thwarted the will of the people by misinterpreting the Constitution. Many of those who are opposed to packing the Court agree with this indictment in respect to some of the decisions handed down in recent years. Especially in view of that widespread feeling, the President's point demands careful examination.

Mr. Roosevelt stated his case in these appealing words:

The Court in addition to the proper use of its judicial functions has improperly set itself up as a third house of the Congress—a super-legislature, as one of the justices has called it—reading into the Constitution words and implications which are not there, and which were never intended to be there.

We have, therefore, reached the point as a Nation where we must take action, to save the Constitution from the Court and the Court from itself. We must find a way to take an appeal from the Supreme Court to the Constitution itself. We want a Supreme Court which will do justice under the Constitution—not over it. In our courts we want a government of law not of men.

No doubt this line of approach produced many emotional reactions in favor of the discipline which the President wishes to administer to our highest tribunal. But to accept his logic it would be necessary to agree, in the first place, that the Chief Executive is more competent to interpret the organic law than is the Supreme Court, which was created for that special purpose and has been in the business for a century and a half. Moreover, we should have to assume that Mr. Roosevelt himself is better able to interpret that document now than he was in 1930 when he was seven years younger.

There is a tendency for these two reflections to race through the mind simultaneously in reading the foregoing quotation. But they should be analyzed separately. The President's assumption that he knows more about the Constitution than does the Supreme Court comes very near to the heart of the whole problem. For it candidly places him in the position of a master-mind asking for new judges who will think as he does.

It would be just as reasonable for the President to assume that he is more competent than Congress to formulate our national legislative policies. Acting on that belief, and in line with his judiciary bill, would it not be logical for him also to call for some "new blood" in the Senate? Of course, the outcome of such a policy would be to make all agencies of government mere satellites of the White House. The President's argument for remodeling a co-ordinate branch of the Government is essentially a part of the philosophy behind authoritarian rule. And it is precisely for that reason that it has produced a governmental crisis.

In our democracy no one official is ever authorized to direct the entire machinery of government. Presidents are elected as the leaders of great parties to carry out programs approved by the people. In the highest sense of the word, they are political officials, sensitive to the popular will and frequently actuated by expedient or partisan motives. Regardless of how high-minded, courageous, progressive and sincere these Executives may be, they are obviously not in a position to interpret the basic law with that degree of detachment which we demand of our courts. If these officials should insist upon bringing the Court to heel every time it decides a case against the party they represent, we would soon have political parties and not independent courts meting out justice.

How absurd it would be, moreover, to have any administrative official sit in judgment upon his own brain-children! The President's opinion on the constitutionality of his own measures can be dismissed as readily, therefore, as we would reject the decision of a judge who had a vital interest in the case at bar.

There is, of course, an implication in the President's thesis that an overwhelming majority of the American people believe the Court to have acted "over" the Constitution in striking down the N.R.A., the A.A.A. and other New Deal laws extending the activities of the National Government. He intimates that any one who reads the Constitution can find, presumably in the "general welfare" clause, the source of the broad powers which his Administration would like to exercise. But that belief is not quite unanimous. Indeed, public records show that a conscientious governor of a great State, as recently as 1930, was unable to find any such powers in the American charter of 1787.

The address here referred to was a discussion of national and State rights under the Constitution. The governor said:

As a matter of fact and law, the governing rights of the States are all of those which have not been surrendered to the National Government by the Constitution or its amendments. Wisely or unwisely, people know that under the eighteenth amendment Congress has been given the right to legislate on this particular subject, but this is not the case in the matter of a great number of other vital problems of government, such as the conduct of public utilities, of banks, of insurance, of business, of agriculture, of education, of social welfare and of a dozen other important features. In these Washington must not be encouraged to interfere.

This distinguished official protested vehemently against the "steady process of building commissions and regulatory bodies and special legislation like huge inverted pyramids over every one of the simple, constitutional provisions." Even though he was speaking in the pre-New Deal era he declared: "The doctrine of regulation and legislation by 'master minds' in whose judgment and will all the people may gladly and quietly acquiesce, has been too glaringly apparent at Washington during these last ten years."

Of course, the author of these comments—today they would be considered anti-Administration propaganda—is none other than Franklin D. Roosevelt. At that time he was governor of New York. Since his arrival at Washington Mr. Roosevelt has changed his mind as to the extent of the federal power. That should not and does not cause him any embarrassment, for any intelligent statesman shifts his attitude when he becomes convinced that his first position was wrong. But his trend of thinking in 1930 cogently suggests that Mr. Roosevelt would have joined with the Supreme Court justices now on the bench in declaring the N.R.A. and the A.A.A. unconstitutional, if he had gone from his gubernatorial post to the judicial branch instead of the White House.

The moral of these shifting currents of opinion is plain. Any citizen or official has a right to criticize the Supreme Court and to expound his own views of the Constitution. But no court could be expected to follow in its decisions the revolution through which the views of Mr. Roosevelt passed on his transfer from Albany to Washington.

In view of that record, how can we avoid the conclusion that his interpretation of the basic law can be readily twisted to permit any extension of centralized power which may appear desirable at the moment? So long as we prize self-government in the American tradition, therefore, it would be the utmost folly to let a President, who is already seeking undefined new powers, establish his special interpretation of the national charter, whether by the appointment of additional justices or by any other means.

IV.

THE BALANCE WHEEL OF DEMOCRACY

Some such tribunal is clearly essential to prevent an appeal to the sword and a dissolution of the compact.
—*James Madison*

IN THE mind of the President the chief question in the Supreme Court controversy seems to be one of economic and social reforms. To the opposition it is a question of maintaining our system of government. Mr. Roosevelt and his supporters believe that the end justifies the means, even though the means employed may be irregular. The opposing group replies that no short-cut to stability, even if it should prove effective from the economic point of view, could justify any weakening of our constitutional safeguards in a period when personal rule is gaining on so wide a front in other parts of the world.

To appreciate what is at stake, therefore, it is necessary to understand the government under which we live. The people are always inclined to bemoan the inefficiency of democratic government in times of crisis. Usually they have reason to do so. For self-government is the most complicated method of political control ever devised, and our particular type of federalized, constitutional democracy is the most difficult form of self-government to operate successfully. Yet the people cling to it as a precious heritage for the simple reason that it has permitted so large a degree of personal liberty and local autonomy along with the orderly development of our national life.

From the beginning our government has been one of limited powers. The experience of the American colonies with arbitrary officials whom the people could not control left a deep impression upon the Founding Fathers. That is why they tried so diligently in the Constitutional Convention to set up guarantees against any possible restoration of such rule. The result has been appropriately summarized by Senator Gerald P. Nye. "The Constitution contains approximately 80 grants of power as contrasted with 115 prohibitions," he said in a recent broadcast. "It presents approximately 20 grants of legislative authority and at the same time imposes more than 70 restraints. These figures show the Constitution as clothing the Government more with limitations than with powers."

There was no thought of hamstringing any governmental agency in thus restricting the sphere within which the servants of the people might function. On the contrary, the convention met for the special purpose of creating a more effective central government than the Articles of Confederation had provided. But the savants of 1787 did wish to keep political authorities in what they regarded as their proper place. The Declaration of Independence had established the doctrine that "all men are created equal, that they are endowed by their Creator with certain unalienable rights, that among these are life, liberty and the pursuit of happiness." This was not just a high-sounding phrase to the Founding Fathers. In writing the Constitution they set up a system of government that could not encroach upon those "unalienable rights."

Precisely this same objective of guaranteeing the citizen against the hazards of arbitrary government by any temporary majority led to the division of powers among legislative, executive and judicial branches. "It is by balancing one of these three powers against the other two," said John Adams, "that the efforts of human nature toward tyranny can alone be checked and restrained and any degree of freedom preserved." James Madison presented another facet of the argument with equal cogency: "The accumulation of all powers, legislative, executive and judicial, in the same hands, whether of one, a few, or many, and whether hereditary, self-appointed, or elective, may justly be pronounced the very definition of tyranny." "I agree," said Alexander Hamilton, "that there is no liberty if the powers of judging be not separated from the legislative and executive powers."

So long as Congress has the right and the disposition to legislate, it can check any tendency on the part of the Chief Executive to set up a dictatorial regime. Likewise, the President can veto extravagant or unsound acts of Congress. And the Supreme Court can restrain either or both from exceeding their authority under the Constitution when the legality of such acts is judicially challenged. It is easy to see how quickly the balance of this system might be destroyed if the President should be granted the privilege of remaking the Court for the specific purpose of obtaining powers now denied his Administration.

Throughout our history statesmen and political scientists have feared the disintegrating force resulting from encroachment of one department upon another. More than a century ago Daniel Webster declared that "one great object of written constitutions is to keep the departments of government as distinct as possible." In our own generation Elihu Root pointed out that "there can be no security for liberty" unless each official is limited to those powers definitely assigned to him. The following warning from his *Experiments in Government and the Essentials of the Constitution* is particularly applicable to the present situation:

If whatever great officer of state happens to be the most forceful, skillful and ambitious, is permitted to overrun and absorb to himself the powers of all other officers and to control their action, there ensues that concentration of power which destroys the working of free institutions, enables the holder to continue himself in power, and leaves no opportunity to the people for a change except through revolution.

To gain an accurate impression of the service rendered by the Supreme Court attention should also be given to the division of authority between Washington and the State capitals. Actually our unique system consists of governments within governments and neatly-balanced agencies within each unit. This intricate system could not possibly have functioned as it has for 150 years without an effective balance wheel. If Congress, the President and forty-eight different State Legislatures had been left to interpret the Constitution for themselves, we should have fifty different versions of that document. No federal democracy could survive such chaos.

The work of the Supreme Court in thus holding each agency of government within its own orbit, until the people themselves order a change, is conceded to be one of the most remarkable contributions of the United States to the science of government. For an impartial estimate of this service there is no better source than *The American Commonwealth* by James Bryce:

It is nevertheless true that there is no part of the American system which reflects more credit on its authors or has worked better in practice [than the Supreme Court]. It has had the advantage of relegating questions not only intricate and delicate, but peculiarly liable to excite political passions, to the cool, dry atmosphere of judicial determination. The relations of the central federal power to the States and the amount of authority which Congress and the President are respectively entitled to exercise, have been the most permanently grave questions in American history, with which nearly every other political problem has become entangled. If they had been left to be settled by Congress, itself an interested party, or by any dealings between the Congress and the State Legislatures, the dangers of a conflict would have been extreme, and instead of one civil war there might have been several. But the universal respect felt for the Constitution, a respect which grows the longer it stands, has disposed men to defer to any decision which seems honestly and logically to unfold the meaning of its terms. In obeying such a decision they are obeying not the judges but the people who enacted the Constitution.

When we thus examine our governmental institutions realistically we are forced to conclude that judicial review of legislative acts is one of the most fundamental principles on which they have been built. Indeed, that doctrine grows directly out of the American belief in natural rights which are beyond executive or legislative control. If we are to maintain a governmental system of limited powers and of divided responsibilities, independent judicial review is as essential as the collection of taxes. Without it the Constitution would soon be a dead letter. It naturally follows that any reckless tampering with judicial review would be a severe blow to our entire political system.

There is, of course, nothing sinister about this power exercised by the courts. In an effort to bring discredit upon the judiciary, some advocates of the President's short-cut device intimate that drastic measures are justified because, in the early days of the republic, the Court usurped power to "veto" legislative acts. But that is simply an appeal to prejudice. The mere fact that the Court has exercised its power to set constitutional provisions above legislative acts for 134 years should be sufficient to silence loose criticism of this sort. Had not the people recognized the necessity of such a balance wheel they would have restrained the Court by constitutional amendment long ago.

Of course, the Court never "vetoes" an act of Congress. That power is exercised solely by the Executive. The judicial branch passes judgment on a statute only when a citizen alleges that his constitutional rights have been invaded. In such cases it has no alternative to measuring the statute against the organic law.

Loose talk about judicial "usurpation" arises from the fact that the Constitution does not specifically authorize the Court to upset legislative enactments. But such a specific grant would have been redundant. For it is really contained in sections 1 and 2 of Article III: "The judicial power of the United States shall be vested in one Supreme Court, and in such inferior courts as the Congress may from time to time ordain and establish . . . The judicial power shall extend to all cases, in law and equity, arising under this Constitution . . ." In addition, the justices are required to take an oath to support the fundamental law. They could not possibly adhere to this oath in adjudicating cases before them without setting aside statutes in conflict with the Constitution.

Modern scholars have engaged in extensive research to determine what the Founding Fathers thought of judicial review. Not all of their conclusions are in agreement. One fact stands out clearly, however: the Constitution was adopted on the assumption, boldly emphasized in *The Federalist,* that the Court would protect the rights of the people against legislative encroachments.

Moreover, the first Congress recognized the necessity of judicial review in our dual system of government. In the Judiciary Act of 1789 it provided that the Supreme Court might reverse or affirm decisions of the State courts invalidating either State or national laws incompatible with the Constitution. Thus the Supreme Court, at the very beginning, was recognized as the clearing house for constitutional disputes. That was an essential step to make our federal system workable. It is even more essential today.

In its role as a balance wheel for our many governmental institutions the Supreme Court has succeeded for a century and a half only because of its courageous independence. Occasionally in its early history it was tainted by partisanship. Everyone agrees, including the Court itself, that it has made occasional mistakes. But its general record is one of remarkable detachment from the whims and emotions that have periodically swept over the country.

Associate Justice Harlan F. Stone has aptly expressed the significance of this record:

The progress of the Court to its present position as the acknowledged arbiter between conflicting claims of governmental power is in itself an interesting chapter of constitutional history. That it has attained to that position is not due alone to the fact that its great powers were conferred upon it by a written constitution. It is due quite as much to the position which it early assumed and has always maintained of independence from every external influence, and to thoroughness and fidelity in the performance of its judicial labors.

If time would permit, it would be interesting to refer to the repeated decisions of the Court in the past 50 years, where, as in earlier periods, its action has shown the complete detachment of its judges from all external influences. Where the Court has divided, the divisions have not been along party or political lines, but have rested on more fundamental differences of legal and political philosophy. And so it may be said, with the support of its entire history, that the position of the Court as the controlling influence which holds each of the governments in our system and each branch of the National Government moving within its own orbit, with general acquiescence in the fairness and justice of its judgments, has been due more to its steadfast adherence to the best traditions of judicial independence than to any other cause.

Should Congress now stoop to the enactment of a law tending to place the Court under domination from the White House, all this remarkable tradition and the security it has given the American people might easily vanish like "an ocean of dreams."

The President's most glaring mistake is his assumption that this momentous issue is drawn between himself and the Supreme Court. Actually his complaint is against the American system of government, which cannot be suddenly wrenched out of its traditional pattern to accommodate New

Deal concepts. But the Supreme Court did not write the charter of 1787 and it cannot speak for the people in amending that document. If a packed Court should presume to exercise that power, our whole system of checks and balances could be expected to topple.

The real function of the Court is to avert precisely that danger. To quote *The American Commonwealth* again:

The Supreme Court is the living voice of the Constitution—that is, of the will of the people expressed in the fundamental laws they have enacted. It is, therefore, as some one has said, the conscience of the people, who have resolved to restrain themselves from hasty or unjust action by placing their representatives under the restriction of a permanent law. It is the guarantee of the minority, who, when threatened by the impatient vehemence of a majority, can appeal to this permanent law, finding the interpreter and enforcer thereof in a Court set high above the assaults of faction.

To discharge these momentous functions, the Court must be stable even as the Constitution is stable . . . It must resist transitory impulses, and resist them the more firmly the more vehement they are. Entrenched behind impregnable ramparts, it must be able to defy at once the open attacks of the other departments of government, and the more dangerous, because impalpable, seductions of popular sentiment.

If the controversy is traced to its source, therefore, it takes us back, not to the opinions of the Court, but to the Constitution itself. The Court cannot take the responsibility of changing the traditionally accepted meaning of that document to suit the convenience of the party in power. Critics may honestly disagree with that tribunal as to what our 150-year-old charter means. But the Administration cannot rationally discipline judges for placing the higher law above mere legislative acts when it conscientiously believes there is a conflict between them.

Only under authoritarian rule are institutions crushed because they do not serve the immediate purpose of the group in power. If the American people wish to retain control over their destiny, they must have the patience to await the adjustment of political instrumentalities by slower and more orderly processes. This does not mean, of course, that the power of the Court is superior to that of Congress. "It only supposes," as Hamilton pointed out a century and a half ago, "that the power of the people is superior to both"—and that revolutionary changes should await their approval.

V.

IS THE HUGHES COURT PACKED?

No one can truly say that our courts have held us back or have ever exhibited a spirit of mere literalness and reaction.
—Woodrow Wilson

ONE of the most dangerous aspects of the controversy is the attempt to discredit the Supreme Court in the public mind. Confidence in the impartial administration of justice by the courts is the tap root of democracy. To disturb it is to tamper with the stability of our whole political system. Yet advocates of the President's remodeling device have been willing to take that risk. Realizing that their demand for a change calls for proof that the present Court has run amuck, they have centered their attack more and more directly upon the integrity of that institution.

This strategy dates back to President Roosevelt's scornful reference to "horse and buggy days" after the N.R.A. had been invalidated. More recently, however, it has given rise to the charge that the Supreme Court over which Chief Justice Hughes presides is packed, and to the claim that the President is merely seeking to unpack it. That argument should be carefully examined.

What is meant by a packed Court? The term

might be construed as indicating that only men of one economic or political persuasion have been appointed to our highest tribunal. But the President would be first to protest against that view. One of his chief complaints is that the Court sometimes hands down five-to-four decisions. Such division of judgment would be impossible, of course, in a group adhering to any one conception of the organic law.

To determine whether the Court is packed it is necessary to take a glance at its personnel. The nine judges serving when President Roosevelt sent his judiciary bill to congress had been appointed by five different Presidents—Taft, Wilson, Harding, Coolidge and Hoover. Would any one be so naive as to accuse Woodrow Wilson of packing the Court? The thought is absurd. Wilson's view of court packing is forcibly expressed by these words from his own pen:

It is within the undoubted constitutional power of Congress to overwhelm the opposition of the Supreme Court on any question by increasing the number of justices and refusing to confirm any appointments to the new places which do not promise to change the opinion of the Court. But we do not think such a violation of the spirit of the Constitution is possible, simply because we share and contribute to that public opinion which makes such outrages upon constitutional morality impossible by standing ready to curse them.

The distinguished President who thus voiced his abhorrence of packing the Court appointed to

its membership Associate Justice James Clark Mc-
Reynolds, who is generally regarded as the most
conservative jurist on the present supreme bench.
Less than two years later Wilson had the privilege
of selecting another associate justice. He chose that
great liberal, Louis Dembitz Brandeis. This record
is the antithesis of packing.

Former Justice Willis Van Devanter, appointed
by President Taft, and Justices George Sutherland
and Pierce Butler, chosen by President Harding,
have usually taken a conservative view of constitutional issues. Still it would be laughable to regard
appointments made in 1910 and 1922 as packing
the Court against the New Deal. Conservative Cal-
vin Coolidge named the most outspoken liberal of
the present Court, Associate Justice Harlan Fiske
Stone. President Hoover selected Chief Justice
Charles Evans Hughes, who often speaks on the
liberal side; Justice Owen Josephus Roberts, who
might be described as a liberal conservative, and
Justice Benjamin Nathan Cardozo, who had earned
a reputation as a liberal jurist long before his ele-
vation to the Supreme Court.

No President is likely to achieve complete ob-
jectivity in making appointments of this kind. But
this record strongly suggests that most of our recent
Chief Executives have attempted to keep a reasonable balance between the liberal and conservative
elements in making their nominations. Certainly
there is nothing in the record of the two administrations immediately preceding the New Deal to

indicate so much as a desire to fill the Court with reactionary judges.

Any plea for "unpacking" the Court must be regarded, therefore, as a crude smoke screen. Even if it could be shown that the Court is overburdened with hand-picked representatives of the "old order," White House mathematics could scarcely make two wrongs equal one right. More reasoning and less emphasis upon supposedly popular slogans would turn the specious "unpacking" argument into a condemnation of the President's own tactics. For he seeks to accomplish by illegitimate means the destructive ends which his supporters accuse previous administrations of attaining by perfectly normal procedure.

If further evidence is needed to show that the present Court is independent in both spirit and action, it may be found in the recent opinions it had handed down before any change in its membership had been suggested. In the attempt to prove that the Court entertains prejudices against the New Deal there is a tendency to forget that the Administration won the gold clause cases, the arms embargo case and various other suits over constitutional issues. In the Alabama Power Company case the Court deliberately refrained from passing upon the constitutionality of the Tennessee Valley Authority.

In the three-year period ending March 31, 1937, the Court decided 180 cases involving constitutional issues. Of 30 federal cases, governmental acts or laws were held to be constitutional in 17, unconstitutional in 13. For the 150 State cases the score was 92 constitutional and 58 unconstitutional. Incidentally, less than 2 per cent of these opinions were split 5-to-4.

The simple facts are that the Court exercised its independent judgment each time it was compelled to test New Deal statutes. There has been no lining-up against the Administration. The mortality rate of congressional acts tested in the courts has been increased since 1933, but that can be reasonably explained by the revolutionary type of measures enacted to deal with unprecedented conditions. For the character of this legislation the President was largely responsible. And it was he who advised Congress to let no "doubts as to constitutionality, however reasonable," block enactment of the Guffey Coal bill, which the Court later invalidated.

With this evidence at hand, charges that the Court is packed against the New Deal vanish into thin air. What, then, is the specific complaint of those who are trying to add six duplicates of the President's legal mind to the supreme bench? Do they insinuate that the Court is packed against the people? That seems to be the implication, but it is seldom positively stated because of the vast store of evidence to the contrary.

It is commonplace to speak of the Supreme Court as a great citadel of human rights. Yet when a critical issue arises we naturally revert to these elementary facts. They seem to be essential to reestablish basic principles that are slipping from the grasp of some political leaders in this hectic age. In considering a step which might easily substitute a political court for our highest judicial body, the man on the street, the farmer in the field and the forgotten man hunting a job will not be inclined to forget the many instances in which this single institution has stood between some humble citizen and the executioner's chair.

This aspect of the Court's record has been effectively epitomized by Senator William E. Borah:

It is a demonstrable truth, supported by a wealth of facts, that the Supreme Court, in instances too numerous to be recorded tonight, has thrown the shield of the Constitution about the rights of the citizen when all other appeals for relief have failed him. When war passion, or mob passion, or political zeal, or selfish schemes have carried men beyond reason or justice, the Court, when called upon, has interposed to avert great wrongs. This is well illustrated by two recent cases: One where three ignorant, illiterate, impecunious Negroes, victims of mob passion and official cowardice, at last found safety and life in the order of the Supreme Court. The other, where a babbling fool, preaching destruction of the Constitution and the Court as the tools of capitalism, found liberty under the terms and by authority of the very things he would destroy.

In the case of the three Negroes referred to, the Court struck out with almost vindictive fervor at the third-degree methods which had been used to wring from them confessions of a murder in Mississippi. The men had been tortured—their backs

45

"cut to pieces" by buckles on the ends of heavy leather straps—until they admitted every detail of the crime and changed their statements, as the beatings continued, to conform with every order from their tormentors. There was, Chief Justice Hughes said, no other evidence against them. It is humiliating to think that only the Supreme Court's interpretation of the basic law prevented the execution of these defenseless victims. But such is the case. To what extent would the "rack and torture chamber" be substituted for the witness stand in some States if the powers of the judiciary to enforce constitutional rights should be impaired?

Alabama was informed, in no less positive terms, that it had denied a fair trial to the so-called Scottsboro boys. Much has been said about the abuse of the "due process" clause. But in this case, as in many others, that controversial provision was used to forbid the execution of human beings who had been denied a fair trial.

We do not need to imagine what conditions some parts of the country would face if no independent tribunal could set constitutional rights above legislative whims. At the behest of the late Senator Huey Long, Louisiana's law-makers attempted to use their taxing power to muzzle the critical press of that State. In the Supreme Court this stepping stone to dictatorship was effectively crushed. It is an indisputable fact that we cannot grant complete legislative freedom and retain the security of constitutional guarantees.

46

IS THE HUGHES COURT PACKED?

While the passions of war were still rampant, Nebraska passed a law fixing penalties for teachers using any other than the English language to present instruction in private, parochial or public schools. A respected citizen of the State was convicted of the heinous offense of reading in German to a 10-year-old student. The Supreme Court of Nebraska affirmed the conviction. Only when the case reached the Supreme Court of the United States was this encroachment upon human liberty forbidden on the ground that the rights guaranteed by the Constitution extend "to those who speak other language as well as to those born with English on the tongue."

We have become so accustomed to exercising the rights of free citizens that we sometimes forget the methods by which they are preserved. Freed from the restraining influence of independent judicial review, Congress might respond to an emergency by abolishing freedom of speech, as it has temporarily succeeded in doing in the past. The rights of petition for redress of grievances and of peaceful assembly might be swept away. It may be far-fetched to consider such possibilities. Yet educational freedom was recently infringed in the District of Columbia where Congress functions as a city council. The so-called Little Red Rider—a clause in the District's 1936 appropriations act—served to prevent any mention of Soviet Russia in the schools of the Capital City. Until the act was repealed in May, 1937, teachers had to swear each payday that they had taught no communism, which

47

in effect meant that they remained silent as to the government of a formidable world power.

With the Constitution petrified, we would have no assurance that "it can't happen here." What a travesty it would be if so-called liberals, seeking temporary advantages, should thus lay the groundwork for a dictatorial regime! Not without reason has Senator Wheeler declared that "a liberal cause was never won by stacking a deck of cards, nor by stuffing a ballot box, nor by packing a court."

The line of reasoning followed by the Court in passing upon State laws intended to promote economic security has been subject to a great deal of confusion, for which the Court itself seems to be largely responsible. It was severely criticized for invalidating the New York minimum wage act for women and children. More recently the Court has agreed that legislation of this type is not forbidden by the Constitution. But Chief Justice Hughes, speaking for the majority of five, insists that the Court did not have an opportunity to examine the entire issue when the New York statute was under consideration.

It is frequently said that the Court reversed its stand in upholding the Washington State minimum wage law for women because of the threat contained in the President's judiciary bill. But the facts warrant no such conclusion. The precedent for invalidating minimum wage acts was established in 1923. A divided Court held in the Adkins case that the District of Columbia's minimum wage law was an arbitrary and oppressive exercise of the police power. It was said to infringe the "freedom of contract" and thereby to deprive workers of their liberty and employers of their property without due process of law.

When the Supreme Court was asked to review the Moreland case, involving the validity of New York's minimum wage law for women, the precedent set in the Adkins case was not challenged. On the contrary, the Court was asked to draw a distinction between the invalidated District of Columbia statute and the New York law. But the highest tribunal of the Empire State had been able to find no such distinction. Since it was dealing with a State law, the Supreme Court felt constrained to accept the findings of the State court as to the meaning of that act.

As Chief Justice Hughes explained, in his opinion, the Court could not be expected to grant a review of the case broader than that sought by the petitioner. In other words, the broad question of whether minimum wage legislation of that type is constitutional was not open before the Court. It had to decide simply whether the New York and District of Columbia laws fell into the same category.

Incidentally, that decision affords a perfect illustration of the fact that the Court does not of its own initiative either sustain or annul legislative acts. It merely adjudicates legal issues presented to it, as any judicial body must. If those legal questions involve the terms of a statute which the Court finds to be incompatible with the Constitution, the justices are compelled by their oath to uphold the organic law and let the statute fall. But their decision is confined to the legal issues raised by litigants.

The chief concern here, however, is the situation which led to the Court's liberal decision in the West Coast Hotel case on March 29, 1937. The Supreme Court of Washington had been more resourceful than that of New York. It had upheld minimum wage requirements prescribed by the State Legislature through application of principles enunciated by the United States Supreme Court long before the Adkins case was decided. This gave the latter tribunal, as then constituted, its first clear opportunity to examine the entire issue.

Once that step was taken, departure from the reasoning of the Adkins opinion was a logical sequence. The Court reverted to a prior conception of the limitations imposed upon the State police powers by the Fourteenth Amendment. As early as 1917 the Court had upheld the Oregon minimum wage law which was essentially the same as the Washington act now pronounced valid. Indeed, there is a long line of decisions that may be considered precedents for sustaining this reasonable public control over the employment of women.

In 1908 the Court upheld an Oregon law limiting working hours for women. The principle involved in that decision has been repeatedly affirmed. New York's statute forbidding the employment of women in restaurants at night received the blessing of the Court. As recently as November

23, 1936, the Court sustained the New York unemployment insurance act by an unusual four-
to-four decision. From this rational trend of
interpretation over many years, a majority of five
concluded that the opinion in "the Adkins case was
a departure from the true application of the principles governing the regulation by the State of the
relation of employer and employed."

No doubt the criticism which followed invalida-
tion of the New York minimum wage law was a
factor in inducing the Court to re-examine the
Adkins case when an opportunity arose. The fact
remains, however, that a majority of the present
justices sustained the right of the States to protect
women from exploitation the first time that question was openly presented to them. It is difficult to
believe that their decision would have been different if the President had not asked power to pack
the Court.

The important consideration, of course, is the
fact that the Court has removed the most formidable restriction tending to create a "legislative no-
man's-land" into which neither Federal nor State
powers of regulation could penetrate. It has laid
down the guiding principle that,

In dealing with the relation of employer and
employed, the Legislature has necessarily a wide field
of discretion in order that there may be suitable pro-
tection of health and safety, and that peace and good
order may be promoted through regulations designed
to insure wholesome conditions of work and freedom
from oppression.

Assuming that this liberal view of the Fourteenth Amendment will be applied to all State regulatory laws, the chief reason for criticism of the Court will be removed.

The most striking evidence that the Court is not trying to sabotage labor legislation is contained in the five opinions of April 12, 1937, upholding the validity of the Wagner Labor Relations Act. There has been a tendency to read a broader meaning into these decisions than close scrutiny will sustain. But they definitely commit the majority of the Court to the principle that Congress may regulate the relationship between industry and labor where it may directly burden or obstruct interstate commerce.

The controlling factor in these cases appears to have been the direct effect of strikes upon commerce between the States, even though such disturbances may be confined to manufacturing plants. "It is the effect upon commerce," said Chief Justice Hughes, "not the source of the injury, which is the criterion." On that basis, wage and hour regulations might not receive such favorable consideration. For in that case the effect upon commerce would be more remote and other principles would be involved. It remains to be seen how far the Court will carry this new line of interpretation.

The more immediate concern is that Chief Justice Hughes and Associate Justice Roberts appear to have been shaken loose from their previous conception of the commerce clause. Were they intimidated by the Administration's assault upon the

IS THE HUGHES COURT PACKED?

Court? Did they adjust their convictions in the hope of saving the Court from the ignominy of being packed? These questions doubtless will never be answered. But merely to ask them suggests how quickly sweeping changes in the traditional meaning of the organic law could be effected if Congress should permit the President to appoint really subservient judges.

VI.

THE VERDICT OF HISTORY

> . . . This proposal to pack the Supreme Court is without precedence in American jurisprudence and . . . we must go back for a corresponding scheme to the infamous processes of the British Star Chamber.
>
> —*Senator Carter Glass*

THE United States has reached a point in its evolution where the judgment of history is certain to be invoked in the decision of major political issues. Our traditions are not ancient. Yet we are celebrating this year the one hundred and fiftieth anniversary of the Constitution. During the last century and a half some effective precedents have been established, and the idea of continuity for our political institutions has taken firm root.

In view of this growing consciousness of our past, any statesman must expect a drastic proposal or a revolutionary method to be measured against the national experience. Before taking a step off the beaten path people wish to know whether it has been done before, and, if so, with what results. President Roosevelt was fully cognizant of that attitude when he asked Congress for the privilege of remaking the Supreme Court. That is why he prefaced his message with a recital of the various

54

changes which have been made in the membership of that tribunal.

The President's guarded suggestion that he is following in the footsteps of many previous administrations was soon inflated by propagandists into claims that the addition of justices to the bench was one way in which the Founding Fathers expected Congress and the President to maintain a balance of powers. It is pertinent to inquire, therefore, whether there is any precedent in American political philosophy or history for packing the Court to obtain favorable decisions.

The many fluctuations in the size of the Court in our early history naturally arouse curiosity. As President Roosevelt wrote in his message of February 5:

> In almost every decade since 1789, changes have been made by the Congress whereby the number of judges and the duties of judges in federal courts have been altered in one way or another. The Supreme Court was established with six members in 1789; it was reduced to five in 1801; it was increased to seven in 1807; it was increased to nine in 1837; it was increased to ten in 1863; it was reduced to seven in 1866; it was increased to nine in 1869.

More careful students of history point out that the Court had six members between 1801 and 1807, and not fewer than eight members between 1866 and 1869. But these are details. The important question is: which, if any, of these shifts gives Mr. Roosevelt a pattern for effecting constitutional changes by the short-cut method he has proposed?

THE SUPREME COURT CRISIS

Violent controversies have swirled about the Supreme Court at various periods in our history. Such honored Presidents as Jefferson and Lincoln harshly criticized some decisions of the judicial branch. In several instances a desire on the part of the group in power to change the complexion of the Court appears to have influenced enlargement or curtailment of its personnel. But that motive, where present, has never been the controlling factor. Certainly no previous Chief Executive has had the temerity to request a two-thirds increase in the membership of the Court for the specific purpose of reversing its opinions on legislation originated by himself.

In considering all of the additional judgeships created in the early days of our history it must be remembered that justices of the supreme bench were required to ride the circuit. As the Nation rapidly pushed its boundaries westward, the creation of new judicial circuits and authorization of new justices to serve them became imperative. It is significant, as James Truslow Adams has pointed out, that since Congress relieved justices of circuit riding in 1869 there has been no increase in the Court's membership.

Critics of the Court have attempted to show that Andrew Jackson had its membership increased from seven to nine to "water down" the influence of John Marshall. But Jackson did not ask for new jurists to sustain unprecedented legislative measures. His plea was for provision of more adequate judicial machinery for the expanding western territories. And if there were any hidden motives in his various appeals to Congress for more judges, they certainly were not gratified. For it was not until the day before Jackson left the White House at the end of his second term that the bill creating nine circuits and two additional places on the supreme bench was accepted by Congress.

Lincoln's tussle with the Court is too well known to require lengthy discussion. It is sufficient to point out the great gulf which separates his attitude on this subject from that recently assumed by President Roosevelt. Congress created a new circuit for Oregon and California in 1863 and increased the number of Supreme Court justices to ten. No doubt Lincoln was apprehensive over the fate of some of his war measures, but two facts tend to shatter any charge that he packed the Court.

First, the prize cases—in which the Government's conduct of the Civil War was on trial—were decided favorably on the same day that Lincoln filled the tenth chair on the supreme bench. Hence there was no possibility of the additional justice influencing that decision. In the second place, Lincoln's nominee, Stephen J. Field, was no sycophant but a man of unquestioned ability who had risen to the post of Chief Justice of the California Supreme Court. A new circuit to serve the Far West had been created and the most experienced jurist in that region had been chosen to ride it. In the light of the recent proposal from President Roosevelt, the idea of packing the Court with one additional judge seems a little absurd, and it certainly appears more so when the judge in question was the most logical choice that could have been made.

When Chief Justice Roger B. Taney died Lincoln appointed Salmon P. Chase to head the Court. Chase had been Secretary of the Treasury. Since he had been closely associated with Lincoln in working out the war policies, the President believed that Chase regarded the legal tender acts and the emancipation proclamation as being constitutional. Lincoln is said to have confided in a friend that that was one reason for naming Chase to the Court. But he significantly added: "We cannot ask a man what he will do, and if we should, and he should answer us, we should despise him for it." It is interesting to note that Chase later rendered the opinion which held the legal tender acts unconstitutional.

There is no real evidence of court packing in these appointments.

The example most frequently cited by those who like to believe that President Roosevelt is following the lead of illustrious predecessors is that of Ulysses S. Grant and the legal tender cases. Embroiled in a row with President Andrew Johnson, Congress passed a law forbidding new appointments to the Court until its membership had been reduced to seven. There followed a period of grave demoralization within the Court, during which reconstruction in the South ran riot, and the traditional guardian of constitutional rights remained silent. In a number of reconstruction cases the Court declined to take jurisdiction, and in the McCardle case Congress passed a bill limiting the Court's appellate jurisdiction so that no decision could be made. The Court accepted this bludgeoning to the serious impairment of its prestige.

Such was the status of the Court when Grant became President. Congress decided once more to augment the number of justices to nine. Eight members were still sitting in spite of the denial of appointments to Johnson. But the work of the Court was in arrears and its members were complaining bitterly about the burdensome task of circuit riding. In passing the Judiciary Act of April 10, 1869, therefore, Congress appears to have been actuated by a desire to relieve Grant of the restrictions it had imposed on Johnson, to curtail circuit duties of the justices and to effect other long-pressed judicial reforms. No additional judge had been requested by President Grant.

The date of this act should be carefully noted. It was not until ten months later that the Court handed down its well-known decision holding the legal tender acts unconstitutional. Obviously, then, the increase in the Court's membership could not have been approved by Congress for the purpose of reversing its judgment.

Although the act permitting Grant to select an additional justice became effective in December, 1869, he did not finally fill the post until February 7, 1870. He sent two nominations to Congress on that date at the very moment while the legal tender decision was being read. It is chiefly this coincidence, together with the fact that the reasoning of the first legal tender opinion was reversed 14 months later, which gave rise to the charge that Grant packed the Court.

But that is not the entire story. Students of constitutional history have recently brought out that in the first conference on the *Hepburn v. Griswold* case the Court was divided four to four. That would have permitted the act to stand. In the course of the discussion, however, an inconsistency was pointed out in the stand taken by the aged and mentally feeble Justice Grier. He switched his vote. As a result the other justices advised him to resign. Thus the decision was rendered, after Justice Grier's resignation, by a vote of four to three.

There is no proof, however, that Grant knew how the Court was deciding the legal tender case when he simultaneously filled the new judgeship created by Congress and appointed a successor to Justice Grier. Indeed, the two lawyers he selected, William Strong and Joseph P. Bradley, were in each case a secondary choice. He had previously nominated his Attorney General, Ebenezer Hoar, for one place, but the Senate withheld confirmation. Here is conclusive proof that Grant had not been given the privilege of remaking the Court to his own liking. The other justiceship had been awarded to Edwin M. Stanton, who died four days later without ever taking office.

THE VERDICT OF HISTORY

The consensus of historical opinion seems to be that Grant had no intention of packing the Court. Certainly Congress did not intend to give him any such prerogative. Nor did he ask for it. If there was any direct attempt to influence opinions of the supreme tribunal by shifts in personnel, it was so remote from President Roosevelt's daring assault upon the Court that it should not be discussed in similar terms.

Historians record, however, that these accusations against Grant, regardless of how unwarranted they may have been, inflicted serious wounds upon the Court. No doubt that is another reason why Congress has not tampered with the membership of the Court since this unfortunate incident occurred. Most statesmen have realized that their chief reward for seeking a servile judiciary would be a blistering stigma upon their names.

The significance of these chapters in our history will not be lost upon the citizen who is trying to visualize the probable results of the 1937 judiciary bill. The prestige of the Supreme Court has been seriously weakened by every suspicion that it has been made a tool of the White House. What, then, would be the consequences of sanctioning by law an actual case of packing the Court, not with two justices, but with six—not for the alleged purpose of overturning a single decision, but for the avowed purpose of foisting upon the Nation a series of unprecedented measures that have been found to be unconstitutional?

If the flimsy charges resulting from Grant's conduct undermined public confidence in the Court, the Roosevelt proposal is sufficient to shake the foundations of democracy.

VII.

THE REAL MANDATE FROM
THE PEOPLE

Why should we not have a patient confidence in the ultimate justice of the people? Is there any better, is there any equal hope in the world?

—Abraham Lincoln

IN MANY respects the most persuasive argument advanced in support of remodeling the Supreme Court is the assertion that such a course is necessary to make democracy effective. By striking down the N.R.A., the A.A.A., the Guffey Coal Act and other New Deal measures, it is said, an appointed judiciary has frustrated the will of the people. Consequently, the Court must be brought into line with the election returns.

The American people are thoroughly committed to the democratic system of government. If a choice had to be made, they would even abolish the Supreme Court to preserve the basic elements of self-rule. Hence, the President has but to prove that "new blood" on the supreme bench is essential to make our political system workable and the opposition will vanish like a morning mist.

There is a widespread suspicion, however, that the word "democracy" is confused in the mind of the President with "New Deal." Some of the emergency measures roughly designated by the latter term certainly cannot be revived unless the Supreme Court is taken in tow. But that is quite a different matter. The mere fact that parts of the Administration's program are blocked by Court decisions is no proof whatever that democracy is being hamstrung.

To get down to fundamentals we must ask: What is democracy? Webster provides a very simple reply: "Government by the people; government in which the supreme power is retained by the people and exercised by representation, as in a republic." In the light of this definition, the President's objective, as he has expressed it, seems to be effective government by the people.

Can this end be attained by the means which the White House proposes to use?

One of the useful instruments of popular government in this country is the political party. It is only through the mechanism of parties that national programs can be approved by the people and carried into effect by their representatives. In accord with long-established tradition, parties formulate their policies and appeal to the people for support. That party which wins a popular mandate accepts a moral obligation to translate the will of the majority into legislation, within the limits of powers granted by the Constitution. Quite obviously effective government by the people depends upon faithful observance of the covenant previously made by the winning party.

64

As pointed out in the first chapter of this volume, the President was fully alive to the dilemma which the Supreme Court had left on his door step when his party met in Philadelphia to renominate him and to formulate the 1936 Democratic platform. There was every reason to believe that he would have to obtain broader constitutional authority before all the plans and policies he had outlined could be put into effect. With full knowledge of that situation, he promised the electorate to meet the issue openly and fairly. His pledge as leader of his party is contained in the following language of the platform so enthusiastically adopted at Philadelphia:

We have sought and will continue to seek to meet these problems [drought, dust storms, floods, minimum wages, maximum hours, child labor and working conditions in industry, monopolistic and unfair business practices] through legislation within the Constitution.

If these problems cannot be effectively solved by legislation within the Constitution, we shall seek such clarifying amendment as will assure to the legislatures of the several States and to the Congress of the United States, each within its proper jurisdiction, the power to enact those laws which the State and Federal Legislatures, within their respective spheres, shall find necessary, in order adequately to regulate commerce, protect public health and safety and safeguard economic security. Thus we propose to maintain the letter and spirit of the Constitution.

The significance of this covenant with the people was properly emphasized in a radio address on

February 28 by Senator Walter F. George, of Georgia, a member of the platform committee. Like many of his fellow Senators, Mr. George took a resentful attitude toward the Court enlargement plan. "An increase in the number of justices of the Supreme Court had been suggested before the convention met in Philadelphia," he said. Yet "during the memorable campaign that followed no responsible voice in any quarter was raised for the legislation which is now demanded of the Congress." Senator George openly accused the President of "repudiating the position of those loyal Democrats who in good faith in every section of the country declared that we would take no short-cut to obtain our worthy objectives."

There is no semblance of effective democracy in this record. Rather than government by the people, for which the President has expressed so much concern, it reveals government by deception of the people. There can be no such thing as effective democracy when candidates for high executive office pledge themselves to one course of action to win votes and then reverse their principles as soon as the election is over.

To say that the President is acting upon a command from the people in these circumstances is to make a farce of party government. As Senator Carter Glass, Democrat of Virginia, has aptly pointed out,

The people were not asked for any such mandate. They were kept in ignorance of any such purpose.

They were told that the liberal aims of the President could very likely be achieved within the limitations of the Constitution; and, if not, we would suggest to the people amendments that would authorize such certain things to be done. When once it was intimated by political adversaries that the Supreme Court might be tampered with, the insinuation was branded as a splenetic libel.

Indeed, Senator Henry F. Ashurst, chairman of the Senate Judiciary Committee, unloosed his finest campaign epithets against those malicious critics who had the audacity to hint that the President might pack the Supreme Court. Since Mr. Ashurst now supports the President's remodeling scheme, the following repartee on the floor of the Senate, referring to a campaign statement by the Senator, is doubly interesting:

Mr. Bailey—I wish to ask the Senator if, as reported in the newspapers, he spoke the following words:
"And among the unjust criticisms which have been uttered, or printed, rather, about President Roosevelt was that he intended at some time—nobody knows when or where—to increase by some legerdemain—nobody knows when or where—the membership of the Supreme Court of the United States, so that his policies might be sustained. A more ridiculous, absurd, and unjust criticism of a President was never made. . . . No person whose opinion is respected has favored attempting such a reckless foray and folly."
I desire to ask the Senator from Arizona whether that is an accurate quotation from the newspaper of his remarks?
Mr. Ashurst—It is obvious from the rhetoric that that is my utterance. The rhetoric alone carries its own proof.

THE SUPREME COURT CRISIS

Neither wit nor sportsmanship can cover up the significance of Mr. Ashurst's misplaced confidence. Having won a victory, the President interpreted it as a license to repudiate his party's promises. That sort of expediency strikes a terrific blow at responsible party government. More particularly, it leaves the millions of people who supported President Roosevelt because of the platform on which he stood with a painful realization that at the moment of their triumph their will has been flouted. What could be more ironical than the defense of such a political stroke in the name of effective democracy!

Examination of the "effective democracy" thesis from another angle seems to be equally damaging. In his annual message to Congress on January 6, 1937, a month before the idea of "new blood" in the courts had been broached, the President said:

With a better understanding of our purposes, and a more intelligent recognition of our needs as a Nation, it is not to be assumed that there will be prolonged failure to bring legislative and judicial action into closer harmony. Means must be found to adapt our legal forms and our judicial interpretation to the actual present national needs of the largest progressive democracy in the modern world.

Apparently the President had forgotten that there are three co-ordinate branches of the American government, of which he heads but one. The Supreme Court has a mandate from the people even more binding upon it than are platform

promises upon the President. A "better understanding" of the Executive's purposes does not
change the Constitution which the Court is sworn
to uphold. Under its mandate written by the people into the fundamental law, the Court must, to
the best of its ability, interpret our national charter as it is written—until the people change it.

But the President seems to recognize no such
obligation upon the Court. Without seeking approval of the people, he asked Congress to give
him a Court that would put a Rooseveltian interpretation on the organic law. In effect, such procedure would give the President the privilege of
bringing about sweeping constitutional changes.
Indeed, it might give him, or some future President following the same strategy, the means of
driving a wedge through the entire American system of government.

In 1932 the President did not tell the people he
intended to devalue the dollar or create the N.R.A.
Enough has already been said of his silence in 1936
about packing the Supreme Court. What new sur-
prises does he have in store for the country if and
when the "reinvigorated" tribunal becomes a real-
ity? Thoughtful citizens are compelled to ask that
question. And once more it must be admitted that
the President has not taken the people into his
confidence.

The uncertainty of the country's future under a
packed Court is the more disturbing to contem-
plate because of the fact that truly gigantic questions are involved. Shall the Government at

Washington be permitted to regulate all business, agriculture and labor? Shall there be a general redistribution of powers between the Nation and the States? These are essentially the questions underlying the invalidated statutes which, presumably, the Administration would like to revive. Should the determination of these vital constitutional questions be left to a subservient Court, the country could reasonably expect to emerge from the present era of transition with a different type of government from that which the American people have clung to for a century and a half.

Most thoughtful leaders of today are convinced that some adjustment of our governmental machinery is essential to meet the new requirements of the modern age in which we live. But that is not the chief question raised by the President's judiciary bill. Rather, the simple issue is whether such modifications shall be ordered by the people or left to the uncertain decision of a Court packed for the purpose of giving effect to the President's wishes.

Throughout our history the people's judgment in such matters has been relied upon. Whenever the Court has gone as far as it conscientiously could in interpreting the organic law, and the people have not been satisfied, they have changed the Constitution instead of trying to coerce the Court into stretching it. Again we are confronted by that situation. "Have we not in good conscience," asks Senator Borah, "arrived at the hour when we should consult a higher authority than courts or Congress or Executives—the people, the final authority upon the question of the distribution of power? It seems to me that a question has arisen which only the people have the authority or the right to settle." But President Roosevelt assumes that democracy can best be made effective by leaving these momentous decisions to a packed Court.

It is not necessary to raise the bugaboo of dictatorship to see the dangers in this trend of thinking. Nearly a century ago Daniel Webster said:

It is hardly too strong to say that the Constitution was made to guard the people against the dangers of good intentions, real or pretended . . . There are men in all ages who mean to exercise power usefully—but who mean to exercise it. They mean to govern well; but they mean to govern; they promise to be kind masters, but they mean to be masters.

Justice Brandeis has even more effectively expressed the same thought in these words:

Experience should teach us to be most on guard to protect liberty when purposes of government are beneficent. Men born to freedom are naturally alert to repel invasion of their liberty by evil-minded persons. The greatest dangers to liberty lurk in insidious encroachment by men of zeal, well-meaning, but without understanding.

No President is so wise or progressive or humanitarian that he can be trusted to remodel to his own liking the agency which interprets the Constitution. Even if there could be full assurance that the President would not take undue advantage of that vast power, merely to grant it would be a dangerous precedent. There are some disadvantages, as the President has suggested, in a system which permits judges to say what the Constitution is. But there would be infinitely greater dangers in a device which, in effect, might permit the President to say what the Constitution is.

Reduced to its basic elements, therefore, the present dramatic struggle for power is not between the President and the Court, but between the President and the people. Of course, the Court would suffer severely from the destruction of its independent status. But after all the Court is but a judicial servant of the people. The contingency which is most feared is loss of the people's right to pass judgment upon major changes in their charter of liberties.

"Perhaps some politician who has not considered with sufficient accuracy our political systems," said James Wilson in the Constitutional Convention of 1787, "would observe that in our governments the supreme power was vested in the Constitutions. This opinion approaches the truth but does not reach it. The truth is that in our government the supreme, absolute, and uncontrollable power remains in the people. As our Constitutions are superior to our legislatures, so the people are superior to our Constitutions." But the President is superior to neither, and he cannot be permitted to become so without shattering the keystone in the arch of our constitutional democracy.

In the mind of the President social progress and economic betterment have apparently assumed a more important place than the means by which these objectives may be attained. But are these exclusively democratic ideals? A casual glance at the world about us will show that there is no foundation whatever for that assumption. Soviet Russia, for example, is working feverishly to improve the living conditions of its people. In fact, the Bolshevists are struggling so earnestly for the more abundant life that they tolerate dictatorship as the most effective way of achieving it.

More jobs, better housing, social security, etc., are sought in fascist Germany as well as in democratic England. Virtually all modern nations are trying to improve the living conditions of their people in one way or another. Yet the form of their governments ranges from the complete democracy of Switzerland to the imperialism of Japan. "Democracy" denotes a method of governing and not the objectives sought through government. Its essence is government by law and not by men. That being true, no President could possibly make democracy effective by ignoring the law and trying to bring about vital changes through the juggling of personnel on the supreme bench. That strategy would be very nearly equivalent to the Ho-tian practice of burning down a house to roast a pig.

Without making any invidious comparisons, it is worthy of note that dictatorships arose in Italy and Germany because short-cuts were thought to be necessary to make democracy effective. "Democracy continues to exist," as Raymond Moley puts it, "only in so far as objectives are attained in terms of its own institutions. We cannot hold democracy as a basic ideal and ignore the method of democracy in the attainment of that ideal. . . . It is the glory of democracies that they educate the citizen in the practice of self-government while they protect his political, religious and economic freedom."

The drift toward authoritarian rule in many countries makes it imperative that the President's proposal be considered from this viewpoint. If continued self-government is our goal we certainly cannot afford to compromise with fascistic methods to gain immediate objectives. For it is self-evident that democracy cannot be made effective by departing from its cardinal principles.

VIII.

MORE HONORED IN THE BREACH

. . . To use the letter of the Constitution for a purpose not intended, and subversive of the whole constitutional structure cannot be considered a constitutional act, although it may be a legal one.

—*James Truslow Adams*

DURING the course of American history numerous plans have been devised to curb the powers of judicial review. One favorite scheme is to limit the Supreme Court's appellate jurisdiction. Another method is to require a unanimous decision, or at least agreement by a two-thirds majority, to declare an act of Congress unconstitutional. It has been frequently suggested, ever since the days of the Constitutional Convention, that Congress be permitted to override decisions of the Supreme Court invalidating congressional acts, when such a course is approved by two-thirds of both houses. Some have gone so far as to propose that the power of all courts to invalidate acts of Congress be withdrawn by means of a constitutional amendment.

As already noted, the President considered all these proposals and discarded them one by one for various reasons. To change the majority rule in the Court would, in all probability, require a constitutional amendment. To limit the appellate jurisdiction of the highest tribunal in the country would seriously impair the orderly administration of justice. An increase in the number of justices presiding in the marble palace opposite the Capitol was decided upon, therefore, as the only means of "undoubted constitutionality" by which the Administration could put "defeatist lawyers" and their ideas to rout without loss of time.

During the first part of the historic debate that followed this decision, there was little disposition to challenge the constitutionality of the President's plan. But proponents of the "rubber stamp" Court bill were not willing to let sleeping dogs lie. They saw the measure, on which the President had staked the success of his entire new program, ruthlessly stripped of the camouflage in which the Department of Justice had so carefully swathed it. One argument seemed to remain intact—the bill was clearly within the powers granted by the Constitution.

To make the most of this argument John Hessim Clarke, a former member of the Supreme Court, was suddenly brought out of his peaceful retirement to make a radio speech. Although the broadcast had been well publicized by the Administration leaders in the Senate, the aged jurist had only one important comment to make: "The single question I am considering is, would a conditional increase in the number of judges of the Supreme Court by act of Congress, as recommended by the President, be constitutional or not —and for the reasons thus briefly stated I think that the answer to that question should be—must be—that such an act would plainly be within the powers granted to the Congress and therefore clearly constitutional."

Of course, this legalistic view, so far as it goes, is not open to question. Congress has repeatedly exercised its authority to change the membership of the Supreme Court in accord with the varied demands upon its services. Indeed, an act of Congress was necessary to organize the Court, since the Constitution makes no mention of the number of justices who should constitute its membership. Appropriations from Congress are essential to keep the entire judicial branch functioning. Should the elected representatives of the people take advantage of these holes in the Court's armor, they could destroy not merely judicial independence but also, in effect, the Court itself.

To contend that Congress may pack the Court at the behest of the President without violating the Constitution, however, is to adhere to the letter of that document and ignore its spirit. From the legalistic viewpoint that may be a safe course to take. At any rate, the Supreme Court would not likely invalidate such an act. So it may be fairly said that there is no legal bar against the action urged by the President.

It is extremely ironical, however, that the President should thus desperately cling to a legalistic conception of the organic law. In numerous cases argued before the courts the Administration's ablest attorneys have pleaded for adherence to the broad spirit of the Constitution. Mr. Roosevelt himself referred to it in his message to Congress on January 6 as "an historic constitutional framework clearly intended to receive liberal and not narrow interpretation." Yet in devising a short-cut to the exercise of unprecedented powers he forgot the spirit of the basic law and took advantage of its technical deficiencies.

In its largest sense the word "constitution" includes all of our political customs, traditions and the unwritten concepts of morality in government which every official is expected to uphold as a matter of course. That point is admirably clarified by the testimony of Raymond Moley, former adviser to the President, before the Senate Judiciary Committee. Discussing the proposed reorganization, he said:

In other words, a custom has been established that fundamental changes should not be so attained—a custom of the Constitution, or a doctrine of political *stare decisis*, if you will, which is as binding upon political officials as a written provision of the Constitution itself. It is this custom of the Constitution which prevents presidential electors from exercising independent judgment after election. It is this custom of the Constitution which wisely limits the Presidency to two terms. It is the custom of the British Constitution that the King shall give effect to the will of Parliament. All of these constitutional customs are insuperable obstacles in the way of hasty institutional change. They rest upon acceptance, and their violation is as indefensible as the violation of the express provisions of the instrument itself. The maintenance of the custom of the Constitution is essential to the preservation of a stable government under which people are able to plan their lives and direct their actions. It is true that the custom of the Constitution changes, but it changes slowly and its existence is an indispensable element in a democratic government.

If we accept that broad view of the organic law for which the President has pleaded, constitutionality becomes almost equivalent to political morality. For that is the essence of constitutional government. But where does the policy of packing the Court fit into this picture? Bryce regarded the idea now advanced by President Roosevelt as being legal in form" but "immoral in substance." Senator Wheeler concluded that the judiciary measure is "fundamentally unsound and morally wrong." Borrowing words from Woodrow Wilson, Senator Glass pronounced it "an outrage upon constitutional morality." To defend their stand on constitutional grounds against this devastating attack Administration leaders have to retreat into a narrow legalistic conception of the document they are trying to expand.

The real key to the issue of constitutionality is to be found in the motives behind the judiciary bill. If it were simply an attempt to increase the efficiency of the courts by adding more judges, any challenge of its constitutionality would be absurd. But its real purpose is to change the meaning of the Constitution as that document has been interpreted by the Supreme Court. The President has clearly indicated that his purpose is to overthrow the views of the present Court and give more weight to his own views of the basic law. Patently that is not the method prescribed by the Founding Fathers to bring the Constitution into line with the needs of our present civilization. When we recognize the proposal for what it really is, therefore, apologetic claims that it is at least constitutional appear to be as specious as any others that have been advanced in its behalf.

Because of the nature of the power which the President seeks, this attempt to violate the spirit of the Constitution cannot be lightly passed over. Since he is eager to put aside constitutional custom to gain his ends in one instance, what could the country expect in a possible new crisis, with the restraining hand of the Supreme Court paralyzed?

By choosing this devious method of approach to our complicated social and economic problems the President has aroused suspicions that are likely to run against his entire program of reorganization, recovery and reform. He has inadvertently given warning to the country that the spirit of the Constitution is of little consequence to him. That is not a signal to throw down restraints, but rather to strengthen safeguards against policies which have led so many other countries beyond the twilight of democracy.

IX.

WHAT IS THE CRISIS?

When the political waters are tossed in storm, the leader or party who makes two emergencies grow where one grew before renders the Nation a grave disservice. . . . If democracy fails with us it will be through a war of attrition involving a chain of emergencies which at the moment could be made to justify authoritarian measures.

H. W. Dodds, President of Princeton University

THERE remains for consideration one other argument that has been advanced in favor of remodeling the Supreme Court for the purpose of changing its opinions. We are told that a new emergency makes immediate action imperative. Once more the forces of disintegration are gathering around our economic system, and unless the President has the co-operation of the Supreme Court he may not be able to stem the tide of disaster. Who would let the Supreme Court stand in the way of effective measures to prevent another era of chaos?

It was the President himself who attempted to arouse the fears of the people with this contention. "Now we face another crisis," he said in his Victory Dinner address in Washington, "one of a different kind, but fundamentally even more grave than that of four years ago." From this general thesis he went on to expound his belief that "in

81

this fight . . . time is of the essence." He is unwilling to take the risk of "postponing one moment beyond absolute necessity the time when we can free from legal doubt those policies which offer a progressive solution of our problems."

What is this crisis? What has happened in recent months to justify the scuttling of democratic procedure? No explanation is offered. That leaves most citizens in a state of acute perplexity. For it is only a few months ago that they heard from the same source that "happy days are here again."

If the country turns its memory back only to October 15, 1936, it will hear the confident proclamation of restored prosperity floating out over the ether from Chicago. A few crisp samples will be sufficient to revive the tenor of the President's exuberant claims:

Today those factories sing the song of industry, markets hum with bustling movement, banks are secure, ships and trains are running full . . . And with Chicago a whole Nation that had not been cheerful for years is full of cheer once more . . .

Today for the first time in seven years the banker, the storekeeper, the small factory owner, the industrialist, can all sit back and enjoy the company of their ledgers. They are in the black. That is where we want them to be; that is where our policies aim to be; that is where we intend them to be in the future . . .

We have come through a hard struggle to preserve democracy in America. Where other nations in other parts of the world have lost that fight, we have won.

The businessmen of America and all other citizens have joined in a firm resolve to hold the fruits of that victory—to cling to the old ideals and old fundamentals upon which America has grown great.

It is more than a little strange that the curve of presidential optimism should have turned so abruptly downward a few months after this speech was made, while industrial and business indices continued to move to higher levels. The circumstances strongly indicate an attempt on the part of the President to invent a crisis for his own purposes. Any effort to prove that point would carry us too far from the purpose of this discussion. But a few salient facts and objective opinions may be of valuable aid in appraising the Court packing scheme from the emergency angle.

In the month of February, when the President launched his attack upon the judiciary, factory employment reached its highest point since 1929. The payroll index, according to Secretary of Labor Frances Perkins, was back at the level of April, 1930. Within a year 1,550,000 jobs had been created in private industry and weekly payrolls had increased more than $62,000,000. Industrial production, as measured by the Federal Reserve Board, had increased from an index number of 97 in January, 1936, to 115 in the same month of 1937. For the year 1936 as a whole industrial activity showed a gain of 17 per cent over the previous twelve months.

A thoroughly detached view of the American economic scene may be found in a report prepared by H. O. Chalkley, Commercial Counsellor for the British Embassy, and issued by the British Government. This volume concludes that "the United States is on the verge of regaining in 1937, after a cycle of seven lean years, all the real economic prosperity attained in 1929 and, in some directions, of exceeding it." "Ample confirmation for that view," writes Mr. Chalkley, "is to be found at the end of 1936 in the actual and prospective conditions of agriculture, industry, and domestic trade, also in the orderly rise of commodity and security prices and the expansion of the national income."

Of industry this impartial British expert has this to say:

Judged by any of the accepted criteria—production, earnings, profits and dividends, payrolls, re-employment of labor, new products and processes—United States industry has reached a stage of substantial and it would seem assured recovery which has been decidedly more pronounced in 1936 than in any previous year, with a further advance in 1937, possibly regaining the 1929 level, not appearing to be precluded by the prospect of any internal setback or even of financial and war disturbances in Europe.

Mr. Chalkley's portrait of the American economic scene is not all in such pleasing colors. His optimism does not extend to "the record of labor, where unfavorable conditions of unemployment, disorganization and conflict still persist." The lag of foreign trade, he thinks, may leave agriculture in an insecure position, since recent improvements have been brought about by crop failures and re-

stricted production. Finally, he sees reason to fear
an "uncontrollable speculative inflation of security and real estate values for which there are present all the elements of a plethora of loanable funds,
cheap money and accumulating imports of gold
and silver as the potential basis of a vast expansion
of credit."

In general outline this view is similar to the
findings of the Brookings Institution published in
a recent volume entitled "The Recovery Problem
of the United States." The unfavorable factors emphasized by these experts include the unbalanced
budget, the current inflationary movement, the
reduction of working hours, the threat of "ill-
conceived" industrial legislation and the unstable
international situation.

Perhaps these weaknesses in our economic situation can be forged into a potential crisis. But how
can they be traced to the absence of "new blood"
in the Supreme Court? Surely that tribunal has
not prevented the Administration from balancing
the budget. The inflationary price movement has
not arisen out of any judicial decisions. And it
would certainly be absurd to suggest that any
obiter dictum from the marble hall opposite the
Capitol has curtailed the flow of our foreign
trade.

The Court's decisions on April 12, upholding
the Wagner Labor Relations Act, completely undermine the assumption that more extensive federal powers are needed to handle labor disputes.
Indeed, those sweeping opinions left the Court

packing scheme without a rational prop beneath it.

Restriction of agricultural crops through federal control is at best a dubious policy. Assuming, however, that the President wishes to revive this particular method of trying to aid the farmer, there would be no occasion to apply it this year. By the time Congress meets in 1938 the will of the people as to federal regulation of agriculture could be ascertained. Certainly there is no crisis in American farming that would justify a smashing blow at the independence of the judiciary.

Reports that the President intends to revive some features of the N.R.A. have been substantiated by his recent message on minimum wages and maximum hours of work in industry. Since this may be only a first step toward restoration of the N.R.A., it may well be asked what sort of crisis can be averted by that strategy? An impressive list of economists, including the experts for the Brookings Institution and the British Embassy previously referred to, bear witness to the fact that our best sustained recovery movement started shortly after the National Industrial Recovery Act was declared unconstitutional. In view of that record it would be rather difficult to conjure up a crisis out of the enforced hibernation of the Blue Eagle.

It is quite true that the country is faced by a crisis. But it is political rather than economic in origin. And it arises directly out of the President's attempt to coerce an agency of government which he has no right to control. If the country fumbles its opportunity to go forward and consolidate the recovery thus far achieved, the blame will fall in large measure upon the officials who are threatening to undermine the stability of our political system.

X.

THE CONSTITUTIONAL WAY

> If, in the opinion of the people, distribution or modification of the constitutional powers be in any particular wrong, let it be corrected by an amendment in the way which the Constitution designates. But let there be no change by usurpation; for though this, in one instance, may be the instrument of good, it is the customary weapon by which free governments are destroyed. The precedent must always greatly overbalance in permanent evil any partial or transient benefit which the use can at any time yield.
>
> —*George Washington*

THE strongest weapons used against the President's Supreme Court measure are the joint resolutions proposing constitutional amendments. By this method leaders in the Senate have clearly shown that the President could accomplish everything he seeks by the simple device of consulting the people—providing the people consent. Such emphasis upon the amending process naturally arouses embarrassing questions as to why it was not proposed.

A number of legislators have accepted at face value the President's thesis that the Supreme Court should be reformed. Because of the vital function which the Court performs, however, they insist that the reform should be brought about by changing the Constitution. If the President wants "new blood" in the Court, they say, let him ask the people as well as Congress.

An amendment proposed by Senator Burke exemplifies this reaction. It provides: "The judges, both of the Supreme and inferior courts, shall hold their offices during good behavior, and upon reaching the age of seventy years any such judge may retire, and upon reaching the age of seventy-five years every such judge must retire." To prevent any sudden turnover in membership, however, this resolution would restrict retirements to not more than two in any one year. And to end forever threats of packing the Court, it would limit that tribunal's membership to nine.

The President's scheme would give the Court a sudden transfusion of "young blood" without making any permanent reform. Senator Burke's amendment would retire aged justices in a routine and orderly way as a matter of continuous policy. Such replacement of aged justices is sound in principle. Occasionally it would deprive the country of the services of an eminent jurist, such as the late Oliver Wendell Holmes, who left the bench at 91. That loss might be more than offset, however, by the weeding out of men whose mental and physical vigor does not last beyond 70 or 75.

Another group of amendments would limit the powers of the Court to declare acts of Congress unconstitutional. Senator O'Mahoney's proposal seems to head this list. It simply provides that "no law of the United States or of any State shall be held to be unconstitutional by any inferior court, and not by the Supreme Court unless two-thirds of the members thereof shall specifically and by separate opinion find it so beyond a reasonable doubt." Revival of this much discussed proposal is aimed, of course, at the elimination of adverse 5 to 4 decisions.

Senator Wheeler believes that some of the difficulties of which the President complains could be removed by giving Congress a veto power over Court decisions. Under his proposed amendment acts declared unconstitutional would be resubmitted to Congress. Voting would be postponed, however, until after the following congressional election. If two-thirds of both houses should then reapprove the invalidated act, it would be deemed to be constitutional. In effect, this plan built upon the idea of James Madison would provide a simpler means of effecting piecemeal constitutional changes.

Approximately 150 other amendments have been introduced, among them a very interesting substitute for the fourteenth amendment by Senator Borah. During the fight over packing the Court, however, interest naturally centered upon those which might be considered direct substitutes for the President's judiciary bill. In these measures the President was offered a variety of ways, most of them revived from past disputes, in which he could assure the country against any dangers that might arise from the presence of senile judges on the bench and at the same time adhere to the spirit of the Constitution. But they did not meet with favor at the White House.

The disinclination of the President to accept any reasonable compromise offers very good evidence that he is not primarily interested in strengthening the machinery of justice. Remodeling of the supreme bench is only the means to an end, the end being a redistribution of governmental powers.

Mr. Roosevelt's eagerness to extend federal authority appears again and again in his utterances and his policies. He insists that "obviously national needs" should be met through "national action" as if Congress were entirely free to decide what are "national needs." If there should be any doubt as to the President's attitude, it can be resolved by a glance at his definition of the "general welfare" clause. After noting the broad language of the preamble and the "powers given to Congress to carry out those purposes" his broadcast of March 9 contains this significant paragraph:

But the framers went further. Having in mind that in succeeding generations many other problems then undreamed of would become national problems, they gave to Congress the ample broad powers "to levy taxes . . . and provide for the common defense and general welfare of the United States."

As thus interpreted, the power of Congress would extend to every conceivable action that might promote the "general welfare." To obtain that meaning from the Constitution, however, the

President misquoted it. Actually this passage—
which from the very beginning has been accepted
as merely a definition of the taxing and spending
powers—reads as follows:

The Congress shall have Power to lay and collect
Taxes, Duties, Imposts and Excises, to pay the Debts
and provide for the common Defence and general
Welfare of the United States . . .

By distorting the language of the Constitution
the President attempts to read into it revolutionary
principles that would make nonsense of the doctrine of divided governmental powers. Nor is that
the only clue we have as to the changes sought.
Judging from the operation of the N.R.A., the
President wants authority to regulate business and
industry down to suburban pants pressers in dis-
tant States. Consider, also, the vast implications of
the A.A.A., the Tennessee Valley experiment, the
Guffey coal control venture and the vast spending
powers delegated to the President. Add to this his
attack upon the independent regulatory commissions, including the illegal firing of William E.
Humphrey from the Federal Trade Commission.
Then throw in his drastic administrative reorganization bill, through which he attempts to weaken
the control of Congress over Executive spending;
and there will remain no doubt as to the revolutionary nature of the changes contemplated or already effected.

Brought together, these far-reaching policies
pointedly raise the issue as to whether we shall re-

tain a large degree of liberty and local autonomy or adopt a highly centralized government with broad regulatory powers. That is by far the largest question on the horizon of American democracy. If it must be pressed to an early decision, its importance makes resort to the amending procedure imperative.

The provision most frequently invoked to upset congressional acts is the Tenth Amendment reserving to the States or the people powers not specifically granted to the United States. The Supreme Court has bluntly refused to take responsibility for altering the framework of our political system. "If the Constitution, intelligently and reasonably construed in the light of these principles, stands in the way of desirable legislation," Justice Sutherland has aptly said, "the blame must rest upon that instrument and not upon the Court for enforcing it according to its terms." A very similar attitude has been taken by Robert E. Cushman, professor of government at Cornell University. In a pamphlet prepared for the Public Affairs Committee in 1936 he said:

In demanding that the Supreme Court permit the commerce clause, the taxing clause, or other constitutional clauses to serve as constitutional pegs upon which to hang new and drastic regulatory programs penetrating into hitherto unoccupied fields of governmental power we are asking them to exercise very broad discretion. If they refuse to do the necessary stretching we may well consider whether the powers of Congress ought not to be frankly and openly increased rather than stretched.

When the Court has reached the limit to which "stretching" may be conscientiously carried it is not for the President to apply the rack. To grant him that privilege would, as suggested by Dean Young B. Smith of Columbia University's faculty of law, open the way for "fundamental changes in what has heretofore been understood to be the powers of the Federal Government, without submitting the question to the people." There is no indication that the people are willing to relinquish such power into the President's hands. Hundreds of thousands of letters pouring into the offices of Senators and Representatives, as well as newspaper editors throughout the country, attest the deep resentment which the President's presumption has aroused.

The issue of government by the President or by the people is thus clearly drawn. Changes that reach deep down to the roots of our governmental system and our philosophy of life can never be safely effected without an open and clear-cut decision of the electorate—through a constitutional amendment. If we wish to retain control over our national destiny, to retain a government of laws and not of men subservient to the Chief Executive, there can be no compromise with opportunistic short-cuts that deny the people a right to speak for themselves.

Since the amending process is so obviously preferable to any manipulation of personnel on the Court, it is pertinent to examine the reasons why the White House decided against it. The first objection to consulting the people, as has already been noted, is that it involves too much delay. When changes of real magnitude are under discussion, however, deliberate action is the best safeguard against blunders, such as the prohibition amendment. There is always danger that a remedy hastily devised will be more destructive than the disease. Indeed, Senator Josiah W. Bailey, Democrat of North Carolina, insists with good logic that the Court packing proposal is "worse—infinitely worse—than the difficulty to which it is addressed."

If the President and congressional leaders feel that it is necessary to secure quick action, however, the judgment of the people could doubtless be obtained with little more delay than will result from the "reinvigorated" Court scheme.

The myth about amendments remaining clogged in State legislative mills for years arose out of the unfortunate experience of the proposed child labor amendment. What are the facts in that case? Any one who has followed the measure since its approval by Congress in 1924 knows that its misfortunes reflect suspicions on the part of the Legislatures and not the slowness of the constitutional amending process.

Congress made a mistake in sending this proposal to the State Legislatures for ratification. If conventions had been called, child labor might now be forbidden throughout the country. The foremost difficulty, however, seems to lie within the amendment itself. Many States do not wish to relinquish control over children up to 18 years of age. Moreover, some of the 20 States which have failed to ratify the joint resolution of 1924 are frankly skeptical of giving Congress power to "regulate" as well as "limit and prohibit the labor of persons under 18 years of age." In view of the close connection between child labor and education, their attitude can scarcely be considered unreasonable.

A far more satisfactory amendment has been recently introduced by Senator Arthur H. Vandenberg, of Michigan. Its principal provisions are:

Section 1. The Congress shall have power to limit and prohibit the labor for hire of persons under 16 years of age.
Section 2. The power of the several States is unimpaired by this article, except that the operation of State laws shall be suspended to the extent necessary to give effect to legislation enacted by the Congress.

Since the underlying issue has been thoroughly discussed, and public opinion is very emphatically opposed to the exploitation of children, it would be interesting to see how rapidly this new resolution could be adopted. Ratification by the convention method is proposed. In that way the path might be cleared for a federal statute on child labor as soon as Congress reassembles in January, 1938.

Regardless of what may happen to the Vandenberg resolution, however, it is evident that the fate of the amendment proposed 13 years ago does not afford a fair test of the regular machinery for adjustment of the organic law. An average of seventeen months has been required to secure ratification of the twenty-one amendments thus far adopted. In recent years the tendency has been toward quicker action. The popular election of senators was approved in twelve and a half months. The Eighteenth Amendment won the support of three-fourths of the States in slightly more than thirteen months. Woman suffrage required fourteen and a half months. Abolition of the "lame duck" sessions of Congress was accomplished in eleven months and four days after the resolution had been approved by Congress. Repeal of prohibition required only nine months and fifteen days.

If the Administration were looking for a key to constitutional changes, instead of a battering ram, it might readily be found in our experience with the Twenty-first Amendment. Congress wisely chose the convention method of ratification. The people had been thoroughly educated to the desirability of a change, and they lost no time in registering their will.

It may be more difficult to convince the rank and file that the commerce clause, the taxing powers, the due process clause and other controversial verbiage of the Constitution need overhauling. But a reply from the people on any specific proposal of the Administration could be obtained in relatively short order. Indeed, should Congress fear obstructive tactics in the State Legislatures, it could itself set the date for ratifying conventions and provide for the election of delegates. That procedure has never been employed, but a careful examination of Article V suggests that it would be entirely within the meaning of the Constitution.

97

There is a tendency to suppose that action by the States is necessary to amend the organic law. But the Constitution was established on authority of the people rather than the States, as the preamble declares. It is reasonable to suppose, therefore, that in providing alternative ways of ratifying amendments the Founding Fathers intended to give the people an opportunity to express their will without the necessity of securing consent from the Legislatures. That objective might be frustrated if the Legislatures should be, in all cases, allowed to determine whether or not conventions should be called.

A rereading of Article V will doubtless tend to strengthen this viewpoint:

The Congress, whenever two-thirds of both Houses shall deem it necessary, shall propose amendments to this Constitution, or, on the application of the Legislatures of two-thirds of the several States, shall call a convention for proposing amendments, which, in either case, shall be valid to all intents and purposes, as part of this Constitution, when ratified by the legislatures of three-fourths of the Several States, or by conventions in three-fourths thereof, as the one or the other mode of ratification may be proposed by the Congress.

When the convention method is chosen such gatherings must be held "in" the various States, but not "by" them. Under this arrangement a uniform vote on a proposed amendment might be called for within a few months after approval of the resolution in Congress. Since the advocates and opponents of the change would doubtless sponsor different slates of delegates to the convention, the result would be virtually a referendum on the issue throughout the Nation. That procedure would be novel, but it would be more democratic than the method usually employed.

Some years ago this plan of ratifying constitutional amendments was suggested by A. Mitchell Palmer, Attorney General in the Wilson Administration. More recently it was brought to the attention of the Senate Judiciary Committee by Dean Smith of the Columbia University law faculty. By this procedure, he noted, the ratifying process can be shortened to any desirable period. There might be some danger of "railroading" amendments through in this way. But the risk would not be great. The important consideration is that this procedure complies with both the letter and spirit of the Constitution, and places basic governmental changes before the people, where they belong.

Since sluggishness in the ratification of amendments can be so easily corrected, we must look for some other reasons why the President wishes to avoid consulting the people. One of these is the difficulty of drafting amendments that would accomplish the desired results without being so broad as to sweep away the semi-independence of the States. Here is a dilemma that should be confronted realistically. After months of debate no satisfactory amendment granting the President the broad new authority he seeks had been drafted.

99

Yet many opponents of the Court packing scheme appear to be actively interested in devising such a measure.

There must be some reason, of course, why no set of words seem adequately and properly to grant precisely the powers desired. No doubt the chief explanation is that those powers have never been carefully defined. We do not know precisely how far the President wishes to go toward reviving the N.R.A., the A.A.A. or other instruments of public power. Indications are that he has not finally decided in his own mind just what should be done. In that event it would be impossible to draft an amendment that would closely fit the prospective New Deal program. The situation could only be met by a sweeping amendment tending to relinquish constitutional restraints all down the line.

The objections to any change of that sort need scarcely be stated. Nor is it to be supposed that the President will ever request such an amendment. For its defeat would seem to be inevitable. Despite their enthusiasm for social security, recovery measures and various acts of reform, the people have shown no disposition to weaken their constitutional safeguards against the exercise of unbridled powers in Washington.

The situation seems to boil down to this: Authority broad enough to cover every activity in which the President is interested could not be openly sought by the amendment process without grave risk of defeat by the people. That appears to be the real reason why the President chose a deceptive course and a devious remedy instead of taking the people into his confidence. Success for that strategy would be a blow from which our democratic institutions might never recover.

XI.

CONCLUSIONS

. . . An elective despotism was not the government we fought for . . .

—Thomas Jefferson

As THIS book goes to press, there is every indication that the discredited judiciary bill of 1937 will be ultimately defeated. Numerous events and diverse forces have combined to foreshadow its doom. Still more important, the elaborate case which the President built up to support his demand for a "rubber-stamp" Court has crumbled wherever it has been touched.

From the moment his extraordinary message was sent to Congress the President was on the defensive. When the Senate Judiciary Committee began to examine the proposal critically, through its extended hearings, the opposition was gradually unified into a powerful chorus of protest. Distinguished witnesses from all parts of the Nation and from virtually all classes of people joined in thoughtful condemnation of the bill. Seldom has there been a more impressive demonstration of the democratic technique in law-making. The result, of course, was to strip the measure of every vestige of justification, and to bring an adverse vote from the committee.

CONCLUSIONS

In the meantime, the Court handed down several momentous decisions, in spite of the political storm swirling about its head. The opinions upholding the Wagner Labor Relations Act and the Social Security Act indicate that the majority is making every effort to uphold New Deal legislation when a reasonable basis of constitutionality for such acts can be found. Indeed, some members of the Court appear to have broadened their views of the organic law. And the resignation of Justice Van Devanter, suggesting the natural shifts in the Court's membership which take place in virtually every administration, further emphasizes the lack of any warrant for the fight which the President continues to wage.

No doubt each of these factors helped to weaken Mr. Roosevelt's position. Yet they were minor influences. The really potent force behind the opposition has been the common sense of the American people. In spite of their faith in the New Deal, a substantial majority of voters seem to be apprehensive over this crude attempt to win a cause by packing a court. That is not the American way of governing. In fact, it is so contrary to the spirit of democracy that it has brought a nation-wide rebuke to one of the most popular Presidents this country has ever had.

That reaction is not strange. The idea of "cracking down" upon the Court for its honest independence finds no support in our history, our philosophy of government or our sense of sportsmanship. On the contrary, it is foreign to the basic American principles of government by law and good faith on the part of elected officials. If our Presidents over a century and a half had thus flouted the spirit of democratic government, the United States might not now exist as a nation.

Particularly distasteful is the fact that the Court packing plan was conceived in distrust of the people. When the President had an opportunity to ascertain the wishes of the voters he concealed his real motives. And even when his plan was laid before Congress its truly revolutionary nature was disguised by a cloak of judicial reform. Its sponsors were obviously ashamed of it.

Yet the drive to pack the Court has been ruthlessly pursued. On the one hand, advocates of the plan have attempted to smear the Court—a direct encouragement to lawlessness. Regardless of what the outcome may be, scars will be left upon the agencies of justice. On the other hand, the President has attempted to arouse fears in the minds of the people with more thought of defending his fallacious scheme than of promoting the country's welfare.

Still more serious is the implication that the President himself intends to be the ultimate interpreter of the Constitution. Since he doesn't like the decisions of judges now on the bench, he seeks the privilege of naming more who will please him. That in itself would be serious enough. But the inferences extend further. Seven years ago the President's views as to the regulation of business and agriculture coincided in general with the position taken by the Court. Now he has changed his mind and wants the Court to change with him. When will his views shift again and in what direction? With biased judges appointed to read into the Constitution anything an agile executive imagination wishes to find there, our whole system of constitutional government would be on the verge of ruin.

Merely to state these possible results of the President's rash proposal is to condemn it. If the United States has the good fortune to escape the wave of dictatorial rule now sweeping over many parts of the world, we shall doubtless look back upon this attempt to pack the Supreme Court as one of the darkest hours of our history. And if, on the other hand, we should unhappily slip into the blind-alley of fascism, historians will have no difficulty in pointing out our most decisive step in that direction.

BIBLIOGRAPHY

ASHLEY, ROSCOE LEWIS, The American Federal State.

BANCROFT, CHARLES, Analysis of the American Government (Revised Ed. 1881).

BATES, ERNEST SUTHERLAND, The Story of the Supreme Court, 1936.

BEARD, CHARLES A., The Supreme Court and the Constitution (1912).

BECK, JAMES M., The Constitution of the United States (1923). Neither Purse Nor Sword (1936).

BIGELOW, M. M., Story's Commentaries on the Constitution of the United States (1891).

BROOKINGS INSTITUTION, The Recovery Problem in the United States (1936).

BRYCE, JAMES, The American Commonwealth.

CHALKLEY, H. O., Report on Economic and Commercial Conditions in the United States of America (1937).

CUSHMAN, ROBERT E., The Supreme Court and the Constitution (1936).

FRANKFURTER, FELIX, The Business of the Supreme Court (1927).

HAINES, CHARLES GROVE, The American Doctrine of Judicial Supremacy (1914).

HUGHES, CHARLES EVANS, The Supreme Court of the United States (1928).

LEWIS, EDWARD R., A History of American Political Thought (1937).

NICHOLS, EGBERT RAY, Congress or the Supreme Court, Which Shall Rule America? (1935).

BIBLIOGRAPHY

POST, CHARLES GORDON, The Supreme Court and Political Questions (1936).

ROOT, ELIHU, Experiments in Government and the Essentials of the Constitution (1913).

SHARTEL, BURKE, Federal Judges—Appointment, Supervision, and Removal—Some Possibilities Under the Constitution, an article in the Journal of the American Judicature Society—Vo. XV, No. 1—June, 1931.

WARREN, CHARLES, Congress, the Constitution and the Supreme Court (Revised Ed. 1935). The Making of the Constitution (1928).

WICKERSHAM, GEORGE W., Addresses (1911).

WILLOUGHBY, WESTEL WOODBURY, The Supreme Court of the United States (1890).